# Illuminated Brahmanism

# ILLUMINATED BRAHMINISM,

OR

# THE TRUE THEOSOPHY,

BEING

An Explanation of the Original Doctrines of Ranga-Hilyod,

OFTEN CALLED THE GREAT BRAHMA.



TRANSMITTED BY THE LAW OF OCCULT SCIENCE.



KANSAS CITY, MO.:
SPIRITUAL SCIENTIFIC PUBLISHING CO.,
1889.

PRESS OF
THE GEO. W. CRANE PUBLISHING COMPANY,
KANSAS CITY, MO

# EDITOR'S PREFACE.

This work was written for circulation in India, chiefly for the Brahmin caste. It purports to be from the sphere of one of the very ancient sages of India, who was one of the authors of the sacred Vedas. In it he effectually disposes of the question of the reincarnation of the spirit in some of its aspects, as well as gives us a rational explanation how such a doctrine happened to obtain so strong a foothold in the otherwise magnificent system of philosophy of that country.

# DEDICATION.

To the Brahmo Somaj of India, and to all thinkers who wish to see the glories of the ancient wisdom of India restored upon earth in their pristine splendor of intellectual power, this work is dedicated by its spiritual author.

## CONTENTS.

### CHAPTER I.

THE ORIGINAL SIGNIFICANCE OF THE DOCTRINE OF REINCARNATION.

The original doctrine of one God.—Spirits come from this Being.—He never taught that spirit return to Om destroyed the individuality.—The companionship of spirits determined by the grade of their development.—When the planet once is able to produce a Buddha it ever after is able to produce others.—India's decline through substitution of the perverted for the original ideas.—The equality of the sexes in Brahminism.

### CHAPTER II.

THE WISDOM OF THE GODS.

The original idea.—The visible gods.—The spirits of men.—The mistake of supposing the spirits of undeveloped mortals to be the wisdom gods.—The deceptive voices that speak from the shrines in the name of the great Brahma.—The Christian god only a Buddha.—The savage character of the early European peoples.—Egyptian materiality.—The eternal evolution of spirit.—Om alone to be worthy of worship.

### CHAPTER III.

THE WISDOM OF THE SACRED CASTE IN ANCIENT DAYS.

The Brahmin caste the repositories of intellectual and spiritual wisdom.—External rites no safeguard against declension in spiritual wisdom.—Asceticism a failure in producing spiritual enlightenment.—The Buddhahood always a part of the Brahmin doctrine.—The sacred caste have lost the spiritual knowledge.—The symbols, mere expressions for the instruction of the unlearned.—The Brahmo Somaj.—Spiritual knowledge follows the law of evolution.

## CHAPTER IV.

### THE WISDOM OF THE DIVINE WORD.

Om the Logos of the Greeks.—Brahm, the god of earth, as a creator of planets.—Vishnu the preserving power of life on the planet.—Siva, the power of death.—The Christian travesty on the Hindoo Triad.—The Greek philosophers familiar with the meaning of the word.—The Christian world in the dark as to its meaning.—The barbaric character of its people.—The bloody theology abhorrent to the Hindoo.—The Om was never embodied in any one Avatar.—The incompetency of the Christian clergy to teach India.—The spiritual birth of the nations of the West not yet fully accomplished.

## CHAPTER V.

### THE COMING OF THE BUDDHA TO ALL NATIONS.

The Buddha state a condition of spiritual evolution.—The preparation of the mother's mentality.—Buddhas are not incarnations of developed spirits, but more perfect evolutions of mental life.—They are in sympathy with the better developed minds in spirit life.—When they pass to spirit life they should not be worshiped.—Gautama, the last of the great Buddhas.—He should have taught the doctrine in its purity.—The reason why the Buddha light does not come to the present priesthood of earth.

## CHAPTER VI.

### THE COMING OF THE MISSIONARIES.

The spiritual light of Europe imperfect.—The conceit of the Christian world.—The East the true source of the religious systems of earth.—The invisible foe of the missionary.—Egypt not high in the grade of spirituality.—Greece and Rome.—The brutality of Romish thought.—The ignorance of Protestant teachers.—They brought back the transmitted light of the age of Gautama.—The missions are part of a great spiritual movement.—The release of the spirit hosts from their bondage to the ideas of earth.

## CHAPTER VII.

### THE INFLUX OF ORIENTAL IDEAS AMONG THE WESTERN NATIONS.

The rise of the spiritual movement in Europe and America.—The opposition of the Christian priesthood.—Their ignorance and degradation.—Their inordinate pride and vanity.—The breaking of the chains of fear.—The treachery of the priestly class. —The irruption of the ignorant spirits of the European heavens.—The impregnability of Christian superstition.—The source of a spiritual influx of a true order.—Its effect upon America.

## CHAPTER VIII.

### THE TRUE HISTORY OF THE CHRISTIAN'S GOD.

The Avatars of India.—The Messianic prophecies.—Joshua, the original of the Christian Jesus.—His death at the hands of the priesthood.—His return as a spirit.—The introduction of Buddhism.—The combination of the two teachers.—The Christian priesthood in spirit life.—India holds the key to the problem.—The true light.

## CHAPTER IX.

### THE TRUE THEOSOPHY.

The religious reform of the Unitarian separation from the orthodox interpretation of the godhead.—The theosophy of Sakya Muni.—The mixture of the Egyptian ideality with it.—The closing of the doors of spiritual influx by the Christian fathers.—The attitude of the church toward spiritual science.—The Buddhahood and Theosophy.—The fallacious thought of the Christian world regarding it.—True Theosophy teaches the ultimate redemption of all spirits through evolution.—Pantheism.

## CHAPTER X.

### THE SYMBOLISM OF ANCIENT WORSHIP.

The ignorance of the missionaries.—The ball and cross the same symbol as the phallus.—The images of the lesser gods.—The true signification of all symbols.—The Jewish scriptures a copy of the Zoroastrian doctrines and laws of Menu of India.—The saints in Christian churches.—The treatment accorded to all who have spiritual gifts by the Christian system.—Its effect in the Christian heavens.—The deception of the priesthood and ministry in the Christian world.

## CHAPTER XI.

### THE ERROR OF THE DOCTRINE OF REINCARNATION AS TAUGHT BY THE THEOSOPHISTS OF EARTH.

Planetary life the inceptive life of the spiritual entity.—Premature removal to be deprecated.—Elementals and elementaries only spirits prematurely detached from the body.—Their magnetic relations with powers in the form.—A good Karma not not to be gained by reincarnation.—The better the conditions the better the spiritual unfoldment.—The necessity of magnetic attachment to earth to perfect the form powers.—The necessity of planets to give a perfect expression to spiritual entities.—The influx of modern Hindoo thought fraught with danger.—The fallacy of all forms of creedalism.—Fanaticism and credulity the chief characteristics of the movement.—Neither Hindoo nor Christian theology of the present age reliable.

## CHAPTER XII.

### THE ORIGIN OF THE SPIRITUAL ENTITY.

India the first nation to develop a true scheme of metaphysics.—The present fictitious drapery of the subject.—The segregation of the Infinite Spirit.—Nature produces through planetary relations the essences of the elements in form.—The elemental theory not strictly true.—Man follows the law of evolution the same as the reptilian and mammalian types.—The sacred character of all life.—Planetary conditions as essential to the evolution of conscious entity in spirit as to produce the crystalline or cell relations of the elements.—The office of India in spiritualizing the philosophy of Greece and Egypt.

## CHAPTER XIII.

### THE FRATERNIZATION OF THE ORIENTAL AND OCCIDENTAL NATIONS.

England's conquest of India.—The light of spiritual wisdom that India acquired in the ancient days.—The influx of the present theosophy.—Its defects.—The true birth of the spirit in the sphere of intellectual and moral purity.—Its possibility of attainment while in the mortal environment.—Religious systems perish when they fail to relieve human needs of the soul.—Intellectual spirituality to come from India.—The relations between America and India in the future.—America the child of India in spirit.—All nations to partake of the gifts of the spiritual life.—Sketch of the life of the great teacher called Brahma.

## POETRY.

The Coming of Brahma.

# INTRODUCTORY.

In writing of the mysteries of the ancient faith, I ask the reader to remember that it has been many centuries since I was upon earth in mortal form, and that in spirit even I have been aware that the declension of knowledge has been proportionate to the perversion of the ideas which I once taught to the multitudes of India, rather than to any special class; but as the spiritual father of many peoples, I have spoken to all races, so to the Brahmin priesthood of Benares would I speak with special emphasis, warning them that they must broaden their conceptions of the scope of creative power, and recognize the universal principles that enable all souls to be, through creative processes.

India has power of intellect in excess of all the mentality of earth. She has preserved the form of Divine knowledge, although she has perverted its application, and from the sacred circle which is now open, according to the prophecy of the Vedas, the great Brahma,* speaks

* The great Brahma, who figures so extensively in Indian theology, was a teacher whose early history is involved in much obscurity, he should not be confounded with the god Brahma, (who is the central figure of the Hindoo triad,) but was a great teacher of the primitive faith of Zarathustra, the ancient Persian sage. From the system of Oriental metaphor, the application of Brahma to their great teachers seems to imply that the minds that were wiser than

to all the nations of the earth, instructing them in a knowledge of the ancient doctrines, as well as opening new truths to their comprehension.

Buddha has spoken to the Sudras, but Brahma sends his words of warning to the highest caste of India, that they may know that the great cycle* is again complete, and the ancient teachers of Persia and Hindoostan are again upon earth speaking to the souls of all the words of wisdom and eternal life.

---

the multitude were regarded as specially favored of Brahm, and thus obtained the appellation of Brahmas. The great Brahma probably preceded, or possibly was the original, from whom the Hebrews took their ancestral Abram, for the name has the identical root word in both cases.—B.

* The return of the period when the spiritual world is to be opened anew to earth, that the ancient doctrines may be declared directly.—B.

# CHAPTER I.

## THE ORIGINAL SIGNIFICANCE OF THE DOCTRINE OF RE-INCARNATION.

From the realm of creative energy in spirit, there comes to the world of physical expression a power of thought which fails to find full significance in the poverty of human language. It is limited in its range of appreciation by the undeveloped mind of earth, and unless specially guarded by repeated explanations, becomes subject to a construction that is often diametrically opposite to its original meaning.

Among the many primitive ideas that belonged to the early religious status of India, was the doctrine of the incarnation of spirit, and among the lamentable results of misunderstanding it is the midnight darkness of soul that envelops that unfortunate people who, by the perverted language of what was once a great truth, and is now, are victims of a malign superstition.

If there is any one blamable for this perversion, it is that priesthood that in my name has taught a doctrine, which as I taught it was indeed true, but which under its perverted form has become a source of the most pestilent spiritual mischief.

I taught that One God alone was Supreme, and the true object of adoration and praise. I taught that from this Being proceeded all that had life and existence in the world of spirit or mortal being. I taught that to this Being all who passed from physical life would return, but I never taught that returning to the presence spiritual of the great Om* would result in the annihilation of the individual or his inability to return to earth as a spirit.

I did teach that all spirits could return to earth to manifest, and influence mortals, and I also taught that such a return would be determined by the mental bias of the individual. If of a low order, his affiliations spiritual would be to the companionship of beasts and reptiles, for I knew that all life of whatever order had its spiritual counterpart in the invisible world.

When I say I knew, it was because in my experiences in the study of spiritual truths I was observant of all the spheres of spiritual unfoldment, and I saw that not only did man have an immortal nature, but that the lower orders of life had their immortality likewise. So I forbade the destruction of life, although for many generations it was not obeyed by my professed disciples.

When I taught of the nature of eternal life and the methods whereby spiritual happiness was to be secured, I found the same obstacles to a perfect comprehension of the ideas that all reformers find in all ages of the world. There were those who could not understand how a spirit could come to earth without being re-embodied in physical life, and there were many who could not imagine that any life could be which was beyond the cognizance of the physical senses.

*The Sanscrit Om should be translated by the equivalent All, or the complete powers of existence. It has been made the subject of much controversy, but the subtle Hindoo mind grasped the signification of the all pervading source of being with marvelous accuracy. Brahm is not Om, but the creator of the worlds, while Om is the ruling power of the universe itself, and greater than Brahm or the lesser gods.—B.

The mental development of the masses then was as imperfect as it is now, but there was not then, as now, among the mental teachers of the people, an abnormal development of the imagination, which has since then led to an absurd interpretation of the doctrine of metempsychosis.

To have cited my ideas of the spiritual nature as a basis for the degradation of the soul of man to the brutal realm, would have drawn from me a sharp rebuke, for I taught that the pathway of the race was upward not downward, and that the world of spirit held in itself the power to emancipate all souls from the thralldom of spiritual slavery.

To suppose, therefore, that in the statements which I left on record as to the nature of the soul there is or ever was any basis for the present theory of transmigration, is to pervert a great truth until it has become a most grievous error. There is one view of the subject of reincarnation that I privately taught, and have often endeavored to impress upon the intelligent Brahmins for many generations, which is this: Whenever any great soul arises upon earth, manifesting the attributes of wisdom and love, such a soul does not lose its power of expression upon earth, for there will ever be correlative spirits born there, through which the higher developed mind in spirit can give expression to its own existence. I might even go farther than this; for whenever the earth itself is able to evolve the intellectual or moral power of a Gautama* or Plato, it will ever after be able to produce equally fine specimens of soul evolution, if not their superiors; and in that sense there will ever be re-

*The great Hindoo philosopher called Buddha, the same often called Sakya Muni.

incarnations of the essential spirit of a Gautama or Plato, although as individuals they can only return through the power of the spiritual transfer of thought, which enables them to register upon the mentality of mortals the wisdom that pertains to the world of developed mind.*

There has been a sad decline of spiritual power of a high character in India by the mistaken ideality of the nature of the soul. All souls are the offspring of planetary conditions, and originate in the concentration of forces which enter into planetary construction in individualization. They are evolutions of the planet, and take their inception there. They are not elementary or elementals in form awaiting incarnation previous to conception and birth in physical life. The planet is the gestating stage of all souls as well as bodies, and the ideas that are now taught as Hindoo theories of the origin of spirits belong to the lower rather than higher schools of Hindoo thought.†

Understanding this, therefore, the moral status of India may be uplifted by the idea that reincarnation and metempsychosis are not to be hereafter taught as truths in the old sense, but rather by their true explanation

---

*This statement sheds a world of light upon the original doctrines of transmigration and reincarnation of the spirit. It is singular that such a view of it should have been lost or obscured, but the probability is that in the lapse of ages Hindoo theologians, like their Christian imitators, sought to improve upon the original doctrines. They have made a strange medley of what was a simple fact in the evolution of the spiritual nature, and we have in the return of this spirit the corrective of this gigantic superstition that holds India in the mazes of error.—B.

†Here is a staggering blow to the theory taught by many Theosophists as to the nature of spirit, and a positive contradiction to

the world can again take from India the knowledge of a spiritual philosophy that shall serve to elevate the nations of the earth above the plane of physical sense, and, at the same time, raise its intellectual status to a realization of the principle that once made India the mental light of the earth.

There is one effect of the doctrine of reincarnation of the souls of the dead that is felt with direful power in the spiritual world of India. Myriads who have left the physical life hover over the mortals of that country seeking for opportunities to become re-embodied, in order that they may realize the promised relief from their imperfect development in the former earth life. They are earth-bound to a degree that infects the mental atmosphere of its people with almost hopeless despair, for however intense may be their desire, they are never able to obtain the fancied reincarnation.

They indeed seek the presence of opportunities innumerable through mental impress of the sexes, but beyond inciting an abnormal sexual impulse they effect nothing toward producing the result desired, and in place of a new life in the physical world they only succeed in debasing their spiritual natures by recurrence to the sensations and thoughts of earth. India has suffered intensely in spiritual declension because of this, and many of its people have really become seri-

that school of Spiritualists who are ever prating of elementals and reincarnation. With the higher thought from the spirit sages of India as a corrective, it is to be hoped that the misuse of these terms will pass away under the light of a truer interpretation of the Hindoo thought. Spirits or mortals who teach the existence of souls apart from planetary evolution need more instruction ere they become teachers.—B.

ously retarded in their progress toward an intellectual spirituality.*

In place of the profound thought that once characterized the Brahmin priesthood in the days when Pythagoras,* of Greece, and the other sages of the West journeyed to India to learn of the science of the soul, the sacred race has degenerated in its spiritual wisdom to the level of earthly cunning and intellectual subtlety, but in so doing has closed the eyes of the spirit to that higher light which should ever be the distinguishing power of the true follower of Brahm.

It is not in anger nor in disdain that I allude to the present status of the Hindoo mind which reflects so strongly the effects of perverted teaching of the primitive faith. The spirit of India has been broken by subservience to the Brahmin caste, but the priesthood has not been able in spite of its prerogatives to preserve its spiritual freedom. It has lost the vitality of the spirit of the thought which made Brahminism the controlling power of India, and, through its mental brilliancy, the governing force of the nations of the ancient world.

The distinct province of the primitive faith was to illuminate the mind of man with all knowledge. Its

*This explains why the spiritual life of India has so deteriorated through a false interpretation of the ideas of her great teachers. The spiritual life being an evolution, and its recipients, failing to obtain true ideas relating to it while upon the earth, crowd back to obtain the promised relief, which nature denying, plunges them into chaos and despair. By thought impress upon their mortal companions, they transfer this mental state to them also, so that the whole nation becomes subject to helpless hopelessness.—B.

*Pythagoras, an ancient Greek philosopher who went to India to complete his studies in spiritual science.

cosmogony was based upon the evolutionary powers of nature. The egg which floated in the vast waters over which Brahm brooded, and from which was born the earth, was only a metaphor of speech which the sages of the modern age recognize as the source of all created form, and from which all visible life proceeds.*

All the transmutations and changes which material life exhibits were observed by the teachers of the ancient faith, and spiritual life, in the time of my earth life, was not disassociated with that life that is the basis of soul-evolution from the material relations of being. There was as much recognition of the feminine nature in creative power as of the masculine, and Brahma, the world builder, had his soul mate in Yutiv or Saravasti, the mother of his different children.

Brahma might construct a world by manipulation of the chemical and mechanical forces, but he could not people it alone, and woman, in Hindoo mythology, stands equal with Brahma, if she does not grade higher, in the work of creating beings having an eternal nature.

For the world may dissolve and pass away forever, but the soul life that has come from its life is to endure in sentient existence through the countless cycles of

*This interpretation of the old cosmogony, as to all life coming from the egg, is another proof that the Oriental world had veiled in metaphor some of the great scientific discoveries of the ancient sages. It is a straightforward admittance that evolution is the method of planetary processes, and the wonder is that some of our modern scholars of Indian literature cannot give the credit to these master minds of the ancient world for their great insight into the works of nature. Probably the supreme egotism of the Western mind, and its ignorance of Oriental methods of conveying knowledge, are sufficient for the light esteem in which their ideas are held.—B.

being. Therefore, let the priesthood of Benares, as well as all through the borders of India, change the current of thought relative to the subject of the reincarnation of the spirit. It will not return again to re-enter the sphere of embodied life, although it may cling to earth with the tenacity of a perverted imagination for centuries. It cannot progress toward the grade of an intelligent understanding of creative power as long as it seeks to re-enter the sphere of earth embodiment, and its purification can only be attained by rising above the conceptions of perverted thought or the atmosphere of sensuality or deception.

Like as the father pities the wanderings of his wayward children, do the risen hosts of India regard the spiritual declensions of the sacred order who have mistaken the perverted ideas of man for the revelations of the gods.

Proud and haughty in their fancied security, have the leaders of the Brahminical faith sought to monopolize the spiritual light of India for the sacred caste; but aside from the cultivation of the mental power that belongs to the plane of earth, they are unable to obtain the greater evidence that belongs to the province of spiritual unfoldment.

From the heights of mental insight in the world of spirit, we see all that transpires in the temples and sacred circles, and if the gods have withdrawn from the shrines, and the oracles are filled with the voices of craft and deception, it is because in the plenitude of power the Brahmin priesthood has failed to preserve intact the spirit of the Vedantic writings.

O, priesthood of Benares, return to the faith of the fathers. How often I taught the ancient disciples the sacred character of all life, and that the Eternal Om was not to be mocked with frivolous pretensions. I warned them that unless sincerity and truth was a basis of their faith they would fail to attain the heights of eternal peace or absorption in the Supreme Brahm.

My words have proven true, and in the declension from that spiritual exaltation which once marked the Brahmin as the son of divine wisdom, is seen the superstitious cunning that gives the Brahmin name contempt in the minds of the intelligent of other nations.

You pride yourselves upon the caste restrictions that have preserved your blood pure throughout all generations. You look with scorn upon the lower castes as unable to attain the heights of spiritual wisdom which you claim as a birthright, but you fail to grasp the true significance of all spiritual growth, for it comes to the soul in its weakness of the flesh as readily as to the spirit strong in the mental acquirements of countless generations.

Did not the god of your fathers speak, saying, "I am the father of all flesh?" Whence then do ye aver that you have a special claim upon the consideration of eternal wisdom, or that to you are given special privileges above the other sons of Brahm, who equally with you are recipients of his bounty?

Not thus did I teach in the ancient days, and not thus do I teach now, but in wisdom and purity of life is to be found your redemption from the power of earthly imperfections.

Sons of Brahma, you are not wise in this. In looking for the return of the ancient wisdom, seek the inner light of the spirit. Dense darkness broods over the nation from the mountains to the dark waters, but India that once lighted the Western world by the torch of a transcendent spiritual illumination has yet a mission of power and grandeur that shall be felt upon the earth forevermore.

She is not dead, but sleeping, and her priesthood are not beyond the power of a spiritual awakening that shall place her in the front of human progress far above the plane occupied by the priests of the Western world; for they have the blood of centuries of intellectual culture in their veins, and when they rise above the superstitions engendered by a false interpretation of the ancient doctrines, they will then be ready to act upon a plane of spirituality that the disciples of the Christian world dare not approach.

O, India, the pearl of the nations! thy glory may be obscured for a season, but as thou based thy civilization upon the eternity of the spirit thy nationality cannot perish, for thy glory is immortality. Earthly palaces and temples fall and decay, but in the invisible guardianship of thy spiritual children thou hast the guerdon of perpetual growth and stability. Egyptian, Grecian and Roman splendor have vanished in the night of eternal oblivion, but the land where Pythagoras and Apollonius* learned the secrets of the soul blooms forth afresh as each succeeding generation seeks as they sought the knowledge immortal at the shrines of a people who never have lost beyond recall the power to penetrate the secrets of the eternal world.

It is India that rules the mind world of Europe and America. It is India that gave them all that is valua-

*A great spiritual teacher born at Tyana in Cappadocia about the beginning of the Christian era. See Encyclopedia Brittannica for full account of his life.

ble in their systems of mental and spiritual culture, although they know it not, and with childish greed and impatience demand a recognition from the Oriental world as though they were the original discoverers of spiritual and material knowledge.

Little do they realize, in their crude material development, that when their ancestors were emerging from the wilds of primitive savagery, the sages of India had discovered the secrets of eternal existence, and formulated a system whereby knowledge of spiritual powers could be preserved for a heritage to the nations.*

Regard not, O children of the Sun, the pretensions of these children of darkness to the possession of a monopoly of spiritual knowledge. They boast of one incarnation of Vishnu † as their god, but you know that India has had its numerous incarnations of that manifestation of Divine wisdom; and you also know that India never treated her avatars with the cruelty with which they treated the only one they claim to have ever had, and which they now aver was a part of the Divine purpose in sending him into the world to atone for the sins of a savage people.

---

*Here the source of that wonderful philosophy which originated in the Oriental nations is clearly set forth, and some inkling of the marvelous mentality of its authors is discernible in these sentences. While the philosophers of the West were bound in a material life-thought, and stumbled at the threshold of the gateway of spiritual knowledge, the sages of India had penetrated the inner spheres of spiritual existence, and were quite familiar with the sources of mind power. They lacked the language to express the thought in scientific terms, but they had the ideas in essence, and a true interpretation of their symbols shows how nearly mental growth follows the same channel in all ages.—B.

† The second person of the Hindoo triad, or the savior of life.

Cruel as they claim the gods of India to have been, none of them equal in savage ferocity the God of the Christian world, according to Christian theology, for their God sent His only begotten son, in order that, through death, His savage wrath might be satiated by the blood of the innocent.*

Remember, O sons of Brahm, that their missionaries are the children of savages, who destroyed their own Savior, and that the mind of the savage is not entirely obliterated in them, although their Savior had no sympathy or affiliation with the doctrines they seek to impose upon India as the work of the Supreme Creator.

These children of the Western nations know little of spiritual existence. They belong to another age of the world than the spiritual, and all they can bring is the borrowed light that once left India's shores, and after traversing the globe has again returned in diminished splendor and colored by the mental surroundings through which it is transmitted.

They have material wisdom and that degree of spiritual unfoldment that pertains to the first stage of emerging from the plane of savagery or barbarism, but they are blind to the higher light of the spirit, and their

---

*Much has been written by the missionaries of the cruel rites of Hindoo worship, but this analysis of Christian theology by the acute mind of a Hindoo spirit must pass for a masterpiece of subtlety in the line of repartee. To preach to such a people of the goodness and benevolence of the Deity who has planned such a sacrifice, and to call their gods cruel, is the height of folly, and the assertion of the spirit that the theology is the conception of a savage people is consistent as well as true. What a pity the people who represent the Christian virtues should feel it necessary to teach such infernal ideas as a part of a Divine system to redeem the race.—B.

doctrines of the resurrection of the body show how little they comprehend of the great truth of the nature and powers of the spirit in the world eternal.

They have, however, escaped the errors of the doctrine of transmigration of the spirit, but their millions who cling to earth seeking to re-enter their crumbling bodies are a striking spectacle to those who know of the sad effects upon the spirit that is subject to either idea. Therefore, I come again, as I prophesied I would come, to say to India to rise anew from the night of gloom and sorrow, and let the light of Brahm shine forth to illuminate every soul that enters the pathway of life on the earth.

## CHAPTER II.

### THE WISDOM OF THE GODS.

In the philosophy of the ancient faith there was taught this doctrine, viz., that the wisdom of the gods was derived from a knowledge of the virtues of the Supreme Brahm. To the latter was ascribed the power of creative energy, by virtue of which all life had its origin in the will of the creator. The transfer of this thought to the philosophy of the West was attended with some disadvantages to the primitive faith, for the inhabitants of both Persia and Greece were crude and savage in their mental development, and to them the wisdom of the gods became a mass of fictitious theories, through which ran a thread of the primitive principles, around which the theories were clustered.

The only gods of the ancient world who ever manifested their presence to mortals in visible form were the spiritual guardians of the tribes and nations that then inhabited the earth, and the wisdom of the gods of this order was often crude and unreliable. The wiser minds in spirit sought to impress the knowledge of principles upon the ignorant, undeveloped minds of mortals, but the latter, in their ignorance of the nature of life in the invisible world, sought wisdom through those manifestations of spirit that appealed to the physical senses; and as they once worshiped the invisible principle veiled in the symbolical image, so they transferred their worship of the invisible to the visible image that came again from the realms of spirit, as if it had in itself the power of creating and controlling the destinies of the world.*

When India transferred her worship from the Supreme Om to the Supreme Brahm she sank in the grade of spirituality one degree, but when she threw open the gates of the world invisible, by invoking the aid of her spirit children as gods, she declined rapidly in the scale of spiritual power; for the latter, although beyond the sphere of physical sense, were far from perfect in knowledge, and the wisdom of the gods became foolishness to the people. That sublime conception of the power and nature of the spiritual exaltation of the gods became dwarfed to the superstitious reverence for the unknown, which at this day marks the religious bias of both Christian and so-called Heathen nations.

In this declension there is no difference in spiritual effects, for the people of all nations rise or fall in the grades of spirituality, not by any superiority of the gods they worship, but because they fail to stand erect in the consciousness that all men are the children of the Supreme Om, and that all are capable of attaining that measure of supreme wisdom which belongs to the children of light.

I am well aware of the errors that have obscured the

---

*This statement of the origin of the worship of spirits and angels as gods throws a powerful light upon the source of India's decline in spiritual power, for to worship a spirit as a god could hardly fail to degrade the worshiper. The worship of an embodied spirit as a god, which some of the Roman emperors demanded in their life time, marked a period of declension and loss of that national spirit which was essential to the well being of the state. The claim of reverence as a god provoked contempt rather than loyal allegiance, and the claims were never allowed by the wiser emperors.—B.

ancient Brahmin faith, and that the priesthood have failed to discriminate between the external symbols and the spiritual signification of the images. I am also well aware that the Brahmin of Benares looks in vain for the wisdom from the world of spirit which once made the voice of the sacred circle respond literally to the edicts of Divine authority, but I wish them to know that when the voice of wisdom speaks from the spiritual circle it is the voice of Brahm only when it expresses the principles of omnipotent knowledge and power, and it should also agree with the ideas of love and benevolence that belong to universal fatherhood and motherhood. When it speaks not in accord with that it is not the voice of Om or Brahm, but of Siva,* or rather the voice of the deceptive minds in spirit that prefer to rule the mind of mortals through fear, instead of that pure light that once established the doctrine of universal fraternity.†

No spirit speaking from the shrines in the name of Brahm, who fails to respond to the truths of the Vedas as they were originally given, should be tolerated as of the Brahmin order, but he is rather a spirit of darkness than a child of light, even if he comes in the robes

*The third person of the Hindoo trinity, or the death principle personified.

† It seems from this statement that India has had its false oracles, who have not been afraid to speak from the circle, in the name of the great Brahma, doctrines that he would not approve or tolerate. In fact, it is more than probable that spirits of the lower orders have appeared in their circles, attracted by the deceptive craft of the priesthood, and proclaimed that they were the messengers of Brahma, or himself come back in personal form. It is not unlikely that the priesthood were deceived by these spirits to institute the present degraded forms of worship.—B.

of purity and speaks from the sacred circle as the messenger of Divine Wisdom. If he counsels pride of caste or contemns the souls of any, he belongs not to the sphere of Divine Wisdom, nor should his words be heeded as though they reflected the mind of Brahm. They are of Siva, and Brahma or Vishnu have nothing in accord with them.

If we turn to invoke the aid of the spiritual guardians of the Western nations, we find that they also reflect the same mental inferiority that pertains to the sphere of undeveloped spirit, for the God of the Christian world is only a modified image of the avatars of India.*

The Christian beseeches the spirit of his incarnate god as the races of India call upon their spirit deities that abound at so many shrines, but the Christian world has reduced the number to one idealized character, who embodies all the virtues of the Supreme Om as well as the full developed mental powers in the form of man. Therefore, the Christian god becomes, in the mythology of India, a Buddha, and corresponds nearest in the grade of spiritual development to the idealized divinity of Gautama, from whom, in reality, the early

---

*In Indian mythology, the return to earth of a god to be incarnated. By some curious transfer of the idea to the West, the present Christian deity is a modified form of this Hindoo doctrine. This spirit discusses it with a lucidity of expression that is quite a relief to the sanctimonious ignorance with which Christian theologians approach the subject. It must be rather humiliating to the pride of the average D. D. to be told his God is but a revamped edition of a Hindoo avatar, but it nevertheless seems to have a substantial foundation in fact, as India has more than a score of the avatars to the Christian's one.—B.

Christian disciples took most of their ideas of the nature of the spiritual life.

But the Christian deity was impotent to repress the savage ferocity of the European peoples, and the history of Christian nations has been a record of bloody strife and superstitious rendering of spiritual ideas that has made the Christian world a terror to the inhabitants of more peaceful civilizations, and war and conquest have been their characteristics ever since their first emperor placed the sign of the cross upon his standards as the omen of victory.

The wisdom of the gods of the Western world has never graded higher than the mental development of their worshipers, and whether they bow at the shrines of the bloody minded Jehovah or the more peaceable Jesus or Joshua, they have ever reflected the inner spiritual darkness or light with which their mentality has been colored. To this day they sit in the gloom of mediæval obscurity in which their spiritual theories first received their gestation and birth.

Ignorant as children of the nature of life, the nations of the Western world mistake the twilight gloom of a spiritual unfoldment to come for the radiant luster of the full truth of the spirit, and proclaim to the world that to them alone is given the monopoly of spiritual wisdom and the fullness of Divine revelation, although all the written words of their oracles, that they have preserved in mutilated form, came from India originally.*

* M. Ernest Renan has ably traced out the connection of ideas by which the Jewish and Christian scripture are connected with the writings of India. Nor are his surmises or conclusions without foundation. This people were spiritualized in thought long before the Western nations were developed enough to have a liter-

As one proof of this, let me cite the reader to the care with which ancient Egypt preserved her dead, that they might again inhabit the earth in physical form, and contrast it with the ideality with which India surrounded the subject of the spiritual life, when the dead were burned that the spirit might forever be released from connection in thought with the materiality of earth. The Christian world still clings to Egyptian materiality in its construction of the dogma of the resurrection of the body, while heathen India knows that when the spirit has once been released from the physical form it can never return to reanimate or have further connection with it.

The gods of the Christian world are ideals in material form. The worship of them is only another form of idolatry which has descended to it through a natural evolution of the polytheism of the ancient nations of Greece and Egypt. In their divinely begotten Son of God they preserve the traditions of Egyptian and Grecian mythology, as well as the avatarship of India. In reality the birth and nativity of all men are alike, but the spiritual wisdom that can be originated or reflected by some has its source in a developed spirituality of mind which has been considered evidence of a superior origin. It is nothing more than a superior development, and, while it may reflect the wisdom of the gods, it has no claim to a Divine paternity, nor should it be so regarded by the less enlightened. When it is made the subject of deific worship it becomes a serious detriment

**ature or even a history. The coming of the Abramic ideas to the West, and their clear connection with the Brahminic theories of the East, show that the Israelitish race is kin to some Indian ancestry, and their religion a variety of the Brahminic doctrines.—B.**

to both worshiper and spirit, and is the cause of a perverted growth in spiritual knowledge, both on earth and in the world eternal.

The voice of the spiritual source of all light and knowledge is not heard directly by any embodied spirit in existence. It remains behind the impenetrable veil of eloquent silence, and speaks to the soul of man, through its own powers, by an eternal evolution. He grows and expands under its mysterious impulses until he can measure the lesser grades of creative expression, as witnessed in the evolution of suns and planetary systems; but beyond all these lies the Supreme Om, that never has been apprehended by the wisest minds existent in the world of souls.

Man can approach the grade of sentient wisdom of the Supreme Brahm, and be absorbed by or equal with that power expressed by the word, but the Om is greater than Brahm, and alone is worthy the adoration and praise of all sentient creation.* Brahma, Vishnu and Siva are the gods of earth, and embody the wisdom of earthly attainment. Brahm, Agni and Indra are each great in their domain; but above all these gods is the Supreme Wisdom, to whom the knowledge of the lesser gods is as childish speculation. Therefore, let the disciples of Brahm lift their souls toward the Supreme Om if they would receive the highest wisdom, for then they are in that pathway that leads the soul above the plane of earthly ambition or pursuits.

---

*This distinction between the meaning of the words Brahm and Om is so important that it should not be overlooked. Brahm, the creative power that constructs worlds, is so much less in majesty than Om that he cannot be said to exceed the ability of man, in essence. Brahm is the world builder, but Om is the soul of the universe, from whom Brahm obtains his wisdom, but whom he may never

It is in vain, O children of the Sun, that you seek the divine wisdom at the shrines of the lesser gods. Like the Christian world, your gods are silent when you approach the Divinity in embodied form. In vain the Christian beseeches his god to appear to fulfill his promises, and you, likewise, will never see the great teachers of India reappear again in embodied form to receive the worship of the multitude, as you have so vainly imagined.

We hear your cries and understand your desires, but we also know that you will never ascend in the grade of spiritual development by calling us back to the sphere of physical embodiment. You must come upward, rather than ask us to descend from the Nirvanian* heavens to assist you in the attainment of spiritual knowledge. We will answer you by thoughts that lift the soul above the plane of earth, but we are not gods to be worshiped, nor are we ambitious to be so regarded. Detach your minds from us as gods, and we become your powerful allies in spirit. Hold us to earth as gods, and we evade you and answer not, for we have done with earth and its childish allurements forever.

O, children of Brahm, rise to become children of Om, and the sacred fires will blaze forth afresh upon your altars. The divine messengers will reappear again in the sacred circle, and the voices of your great teachers will be heard from the inner shrines, giving anew the greater and grander truths concerning the soul's eternal destiny.

hope to equal. Christian theology expresses the essential ideas of creator, preserver and divine companionship in its trinity, but fails to comprehend the methods of either.

*The highest realm of spiritual existence in the future life. The abode of the great philosophers and purified spirits of earth.

# CHAPTER III.

## THE WISDOM OF THE SACRED CASTE IN THE ANCIENT DAYS.

When I think of the glories of the ancient doctrines of India and the height of her attainments in the mental world, I am loth to witness the declension of that wisdom that once made her the envy of the surrounding nations of the earth

To be a Brahmin was to be devoted to the consideration and attainment of the highest spiritual wisdom. The garments of white, in which the form was ever to be clothed, were symbolical of that illuminating purity of character that belonged to the sphere of perfect mental and moral unfoldment. There was a difference in degree of wisdom between the Brahmin and the lower castes, but there was not that disregard of the importance or esteem, in which all souls should be held who possess the nature of immortal beings, that has since marked the decline of the primitive ideality of the ancient faith.

The declension began with the substitution of external rites and ceremonies for the cultivation of the finer qualities of the spiritual nature It is hard for the dwarfed mentality of a perverted imagination to realize this, but no soul can attain to spiritual wisdom that neglects the foundation principle of humility of spirit.

Therefore, the mind of any class or caste that fails to realize this remains upon a lower plane of spiritual unfoldment than the soul that thankfully rejoices in the coming of light to any mind, even if of the lower castes, for the light of spiritual life follows a law of its own when it touches the nature of any soul upon earth. It does not deflect from a straightforward course of procedure, but by the law of spiritual and mental evolution, it illuminates the soul of the recipient with that divine enlightenment that has been a source of mystery to the less developed spirit.

Here was the beginning of that substitution of ascetic mortification of the flesh that the spirit might obtain a forced growth of spiritual perception, but it proved abortive in the majority of cases, for the spirit must have its natural evolution as well as the body, and forced growth in either ends in distorted instead of symmetrical results.*

The mentality of the sacred caste deteriorated under the severe code of physical discipline, and the wisdom of the wise became foolishness through the vain efforts to approach the spiritual world by the systematic suppression of the natural methods of evolutionary unfoldment. The Brahmin caste did, indeed, become famous for its external rites of sanctity, but it was too often external only, for the natural functions of the body, being repressed in their legitimate channels of

*This is a significant rebuke to the ignorance and fanaticism preached in Christian nations as gospel truth. To prate of the danger of delay, or to teach that the eternal destiny of the spirit is dependent upon a mystical theory of theological imbecility, is the weakness of the least intelligent advocates of the Christian system, but here a spirit who has lived in both worlds declares it to be a necessity of evolution that the spirit should have time to perfect its powers ere it can reflect the ultimate design of its existence. With an eternity to work out its redemption, the soul can hardly miss its final evolution from the power of adverse conditions.—B.

action, turned themselves into the pathway of perverted, although secret, gratification, and the moral nature suffered deeply in its most private and sacred relations.

The consequences of this perversion of the mental and physical laws of being were soon manifest in the declining mental and spiritual power of the priesthood, for in place of the exalted concepts of the ideas that had been transmitted through the medium of written language came a distorted and mythical interpretation of the symbols that once served to illustrate the pure ideality of an unperverted imagination.

The sacred caste declined in spirituality, and substituted for that purity of soul which belongs to an undefiled nature the sanctimonous hypocrisy which served to veil the inner corruption from the physical sight and by alliance with arbitrary force held its power over the other castes, although it could not compete with that more subtle power of spirit which was able to penetrate the more teachable intellect of the Sudras, and which lit up their souls with the transcendent glory that ever after made the Buddhists the modifying, if not really controlling, power of Indian spirituality.

It is claimed by the Christian world that Buddha's light has been extinguished in Hindoostan, and that the country is submerged in the grossest forms of idol worship; but I would say that the coming of the Buddhas was always a part of the Brahmin doctrines, and the only error that the priesthood of this age holds concerning it is, that the Buddhas must come from the Sacred Order; for, although they might come from it as well as elsewhere, they are not confined to any class, nor have they ever been. It was not so taught by the ancient writers, and the assumption of it as a condition of reliable authority in attaining the Buddhahood is on a par with the Christian dogma, that those only who believe in their avatar have any chance of final happiness in the life eternal.

Neither Brahmin nor Christian has supreme jurisdiction in the world of soul life, and their attempts to monopolize the principles of eternal existence in behalf of their castes or creeds is destined to ignominious failure. The Supreme Om has so arranged the course of spiritual evolution that even Brahm cannot prevent the attainment of human happiness by all mankind, should he so desire; but Brahm is not exclusive in his dominion of the world, nor did he ever teach that he held one race in abhorrence or another in esteem. Rather did he teach all that by observance of the law of life all should attain to wisdom and goodness, although he spoke warning words to those who should live in violation of the decrees of purity and benevolence.

The ancient teachers of the Brahmin faith understood this and obeyed the precepts, but their degenerate descendants, by a perverted interpretation of the symbols, lost the sacred knowledge, and in vain have substituted for it the wisdom of man in the lower state of mental growth, instead of that exalted spiritual condition by which spiritual discernment of ideas becomes a possibility.

Through this declension the modern priesthood has failed to read the symbols aright, and the wisdom of the ancient doctrines has become obscured by absurd tales of metempsychosis, which excite the derision of the unlearned as well as the contempt of the disciples of evolutionary thought. The sons of Brahma know that imagery and symbols are for the unlearned in the inner life, not to be regarded as objects of adoration and praise by the minds of the wise and intelligent.

Nor should the doctrines that were veiled under the figurative expressions of transmigration be literally rendered as expressive of spiritual existence, but as the metaphorical language in which the Oriental mind loves to convey the great truths that pertain to the life of the soul. I should indeed be worthy of the scorn and derision with which the Christian world regards the intelligence that conceived the absurd cycle of endless rounds of incarnation until absorption in Brahm annihilates the individuality, had I ever really taught such a doctrine; but like the fate that befalls all the great reforms in the ideal world of mind, the pure doctrine of the spiritual nature has had a distorted and perverted translation from its primitive significance, and the wiser minds in India are now transmitting a purer interpretation of its original meaning.

The Brahmo Somaj is nearer the original thought of the great founder of the Brahmin faith than any other sect in India, but it needs to add to the mental concepts of the spiritual world a recognition of its great influence upon the mentality of earth through the transmission of thought by direct transfer, and that the grade of the thought is an index of the degree of mental unfoldment of the spirit of the thinker.

It is right in rejecting the principle of avatarship and abolition of caste as essential to a knowledge of the truth, but it should also enlist the sympathies and co-operation of the enlightened of all races by announcing to the world its true position on the questions of spiritual enlightenment, and the availibility of ancient as well as modern—means to establish a fraternization of spiritual thought throughout the earth.

The Christian world clings to the avatar idea because the Christian theologian is upon the plane of spiritual childhood, but the mature mentality of the Brahmo Somaj rejects the childish conceptions of the orthodox Brahmin or Christian as literal truth, and relegates the ideas of both to the undeveloped period of the race, when the influx of spiritual light was considered to be the evidence of supernatural wisdom or favor.

The wisdom of the ancient teachers of India always rejected the idea of avatarship as ordinarily understood. None of them, while in the mortal state, claimed to be incarnations of Vishnu, or the Divine-Wisdom. Their apotheosis came after their transfer to the spiritual world, and generally after several generations had passed away from earth. Then arose their worship by the priesthood, who sank in spiritual declension in just the proportion that they falsified the original doctrines, and thus the great ideas of the enlightened teachers lost their power through the false construction placed upon them by the spiritually undeveloped.*

For in all nations this principle holds good, that

*India has followed the same pathway that Christian nations are now traversing. The apotheosis of Jesus or Joshua took place several centuries after his transition from earth, and the pagan nations of the Roman empire furnished the bulk of his disciples. The whole body of his followers became subservient to a priesthood that taught anything they chose as gospel, and for many centuries the European world went into the densest spiritual darkness. Even yet the light in the Christian world is of the sun shining in a fog rather than with uninterrupted rays, and its teachers deal with spiritual ideas outside of their creeds as though they were dangerous.—B.

spiritual knowledge follows the same law of evolutionary growth that pertains to physical form in the mortal life. There has to be its periods of conception, gestation and birth, and until the soul of man has passed these periods it can have no knowledge of spirituality of a high or even low degree. In many natures, there is no development of spiritual life above the plane of feeling during earthly life. Hearing and sight are dormant, and the spiritual senses are confined to one channel of perception only. They can feel the great waves of pulsating power that reach them from the world eternal, but they cannot correct a false impression that may be produced by this sensation, and from this fact alone the world's great superstitions proceed in countless variety of forms.

Spiritual knowledge that comes by feeling is about as high in the grade as the mentality emerging from the savage plane can perceive, and the interpretation of its influence will be expressed in a savage manner. The people of Christian nations are marked examples of this form of spiritual development, for they still worship a savage god, whom they suppose to be the parent of a merciful and benevolent son, who died to propitiate the father's savage and revengeful disposition toward the human race. The people of the Christian world are spiritual savages, save where the mild and beneficent ideas of the great Indian teacher, Gautama, the Buddha, have been accepted and practiced; but the lingering superstitions of the savage mind still haunt their imagination, and they regard every manifestation from the world of spirit in this age to be of Satanic origin if it appeals to other senses than that of feeling.

The ignorance of the Christian clergy concerning spiritual matters is more dense than that of India, but the conceit of their half-developed minds is a striking comment upon the efficacy of their system to save themselves from the imaginary wrath of an imaginary god.* As they were never in any danger of soul or body, except what they themselves have devised as existing in mind, it is not strange that a change of mental conception of their god should be hailed by them as evidence of having obtained favor with him, and it is often paraded before the world as a manifest token of spiritual acceptance by him.

This highest wisdom of the Christian was as familiar to the ancient sages of India as the presence of the spiritual world in the sacred circle of the temples. But the Christian world has no recognition of the latter evidence, and sinks in the scale of perfected spiritual power, although it has some in its ranks who dimly sense the existence of a more exalted condition of attainment than their present status. They not only feel the presence and power of the spiritual world, but the sense of hearing is developed to a remarkable degree, and the voice of the unseen thinker reaches their inner power of soul, adding to the sense of feeling the faculty of hearing, and thus the spirit has a new source

*Here the spiritual teacher of the Orient expresses an idea that is quite in consonance with the developed thought of Europe or America. The enlightened mentality of the race instinctively rejects the crude theological definitions of the mediæval ages, and refuses to be bound by them, although they are still taught in the seminaries and schools of theological training. Why the West should still feel bound by the creeds of savage Europe or barbaric Asia is a mystery, except for the lack of a more perfect development in knowledge of spiritual laws.—B.

of mental and spiritual enlightenment. If to this should come the evolution of spiritual sight and the vision be perfect, then the possessor of these powers becomes a Buddha, or spiritual sage, able to look into the invisible world and to perceive the secret causes and workings of the great forces that underlie all manifestation of being.

To become a Buddha was the aim of the ancient religious discipline of the Brahmin school, but the attainment of the Buddha state by the practice of ascetic rites, or the undue repression of the physical senses, was never as successful as the primitive disciples of that school of thought hoped it would be. Sometimes, indeed, the severe discipline of the body opened the spiritual vision prematurely, and permitted the neophyte in spiritual wisdom to perceive some of the lower spheres of spiritual life, which were mistaken for evidences of spiritual wisdom; but the greater knowledge of spiritual truths never came to the seekers for it in this direction, for spiritual wisdom, like its earthly prototype, comes by mental growth, and not by violent stimulus or repression of any department of individual experiences.*

The Brahmins of later ages and the priesthood of the

* Here again is an idea worthy of consideration by the students of theosophical and esoteric thought. To force the soul from its balance by forced stimulation, or to repress its powers in a proper exercise of them in any natural manner, has ever proven detrimental rather than beneficial to the practitioner of the ascetic rites. A true growth is always symmetrical and a false stimulus can only produce distortion. The fakirs and other superstitious devotees of India at this age are the best evidence possible of the wide divergence from the primitive simplicity of the ancient teachers.—B.

Christian world, who seek spiritual enlightenment of a high order through the cultivation of asceticism, miss the aim of their ambition, and enter the spiritual world shorn of their power to appreciate its higher grades of thought, and are obliged to remain upon the plane of earth until they learn the great lessons of spiritual unfoldment through obedience to the spirit of natural laws.

This lesson is the most difficult for either the Brahmin or Christian priesthood to learn, for each imagines itself to be specially chosen by the Supreme Creator for an example of the Divine Wisdom upon the earth, and neither of them really have any claim by virtue of their order to any consideration by the Supreme Creator above the other castes or classes of men.

I emphatically taught that Brahm was no respecter of persons and that Om was the father of all that inhabited the worlds, but I never authorized by word or deed the idea that the followers of Brahm were to have any higher privileges than Om bestowed upon all that obeyed the sacred laws. I did teach that the sons of Brahm should have the wisdom that belonged to the sacred order, which was to ever hold the truth in purity and bestow it upon the children of men. I declared that the light should never be quenched in India; and if it declined in power I would come again to re-establish its pristine glory, and through Capilya and Gautama I fulfilled the prophecy; but the priesthood failed to understand them, as they fail to comprehend now that all light of a spiritual character comes not from the individual who bears it to men, but through the mentality which, as an illuminated reflector, radiates the spiritual glory to the darkened minds of earth.

Therefore, I come again in this age, speaking the words of warning and truth to the highest caste in India, to no longer look for the reappearance of the ancient teachers in bodily form through reincarnation of the spirit, but to heed the words of spiritual truth that come from all sources that reflect the ancient wisdom; for the time has come when a knowledge of spiritual truths is to be again bestowed upon earth without reference or regard to the ignorance or variety of the religious orders there that may vainly imagine they have a monopoly of spiritual revelation.

The Christian world rejects the doctrines of spirituality that do not conform to the ideas of its fictitious god and remains in spiritual darkness, but its condition is not so bad as the disciples of Brahm who have ever been taught that the doors of the spiritual world have never been closed, yet who find that they have often knocked in vain at its portals.

You have been answered, O children of Brahm, according to the answer you have given to the children of earth; for in your pride of ancestry and regard for the external observance of the doctrines, you have become exclusive in your thoughts; and despising others whose souls were as precious in the sight of Brahm as your own, you have been excluded from the evidence of that higher spiritual power that governs the universe.

In darkness you have seen the sun of India sink beyond the dark waters to reappear and illuminate the people of the Western nations with the brilliancy of a new Divine Revelation. For to these nations the light of ancient India has again arisen, and their people are rejoicing in the splendor of a new spiritual philosophy that transcends anything ever taught in their sacred books.

They appreciate its value, for to many of them it has come with the power of divine life, and is lifting their souls far above the plane of sordid materiality with which Christian dogma had depicted the eternal world. Their priesthood, indeed, refuse to receive the beneficial results of this great illumination; but the people of Europe and America, for the first time since the formulation of their religious system, are becoming enlightened as to the nature of the soul and the laws governing its eternal destiny. They will become the children of Om, as well as of Brahm, for to their material development they are to add the next great step in their evolution, viz., the knowledge and power of the eternal world as an ally to their earthly existence. To them the sacred circle has become almost a discarded phase of spiritual evidence, and they seek the higher knowledge of the spirit that reflects the wisdom of ages of experience in the life immortal.

O, India, that has taught the nations the wisdom of the Divine Word, arise again from thy lethargy, and let the sons of Brahm lead the way to the mental illumination of all thy children. Dwell no longer in the darkness of the past ages, and let the altars of Siva be abandoned forever. He is not the angel of death, but the harbinger of life eternal. There is not a possibility of any soul becoming eternally lost, for the great Om has provided for the redemption and preservation of all the children of earth.

Teach no longer that the soul cannot escape a ceaseless round of transmigrations ere it can be absorbed in

Brahm, for it needs no other incarnation than its first to become capable of existence in spirit, and when it has perfected itself in knowledge to the degree of the intelligence of the great world builder, it can with Brahm create and govern a world and yet maintain its separate individual existence forever.

Let the followers of Vishnu and Siva cease to call upon either for spiritual aid, for to neither has there any power been given, and they are only expressions of principles that imperfect mentality has deified as persons. Even Brahm, the creator of worlds, can only answer prayer in accord with the will of Om, to whom he is subject, and prayer addressed to him may be in vain. But, if you must have the embodied form of language to convey thought to the less developed mind, pray to none less in power than Brahm, who will answer you by inspiring you with the wisdom of the ancient teachers, and to their knowledge add that which they have learned since their transition to the world eternal.

We will come as his messengers, and in earthly language record the ideas that pertain to the world spiritual, making plain that which hitherto has been a mystery, and bringing to earth again the wisdom of the ancient sages of India.

# CHAPTER IV.

## THE WISDOM OF THE DIVINE WORD.

In the sacred Scriptures of the Christian nations is a paragraph that has been a mystery to their most learned teachers, for in its translation to the Western language the significance of it was purposely veiled by the ancient sages of Greece

That word which was taught to the Greek sages of the Alexandrian school was the sacred title Om, by which the governing power of the universe was designated in the ancient Sanscrit In the definition of the lower intelligences that were ascribed to the spiritual rulers of the world, Brahm meant the god of earth as a creator of the planets, while Vishnu represented the preserving power that held planetary forms in existence for a season. Siva, to whom all physical life was subject, was the destroyer, and as his power was equal with that of both Brahm and Vishnu, he became a part of the Hindoo triad, which still is worshiped in the symbols (three in one), to the disapprobation of the Christian world, that has copied it in all essential points, save that it has removed Siva to the position of an antagonist to both Brahm and Vishnu, and substituted the word Holy Spirit in his place. Siva has become in Christian mythology, Satan or adversary, and is regarded as supreme over the earth through having the power of death, and the early Christian fathers labored hard, in their ignorance of the true interpretation of the term, to represent the final destruction of Siva or Satan by the power of their Christ.*

Hence Christian theologians have ever been at war with any interpretation of Indian thought that would have shed light upon the origin of their theories, for long before the nations surrounding the Mediterranean sea were enlightened above the plane of savages, the sages of Persia and India had solved the problems of spiritual existence in the next sphere above the plane of earth.

The Greek philosophers, to whom the Sacred Word was explained, understood it quite perfectly, but the lower orders of the religious teachers could not comprehend the existence of an impersonal power that transcended the authority of any embodied form, and so they mutilated the philosophic teachings of the ancient doctrines, and inserted the idea that the Word was made flesh and dwelt among men. This was copying the Hindoo doctrine of the avatars, but they carried it further than any Indian teacher ever thought of

* This interpretation of the Hindoo triad solves the problem of the symbols, in perfect accord with the facts at issue as to the origin of the Christian trinity. In the dense ignorance of the early Christian priesthood the symbol of death was taken from the triune powers and placed in antagonism to them, while the motherhood of divinity was placed in its stead. The Catholic church attribute the immaculate conception to Mary, the same as to Jesus, and by right the trinity should be Father, Son and Holy Mother. As Christ stands for Vishnu in the Hindoo cult, so Satan is the equivalent of Sivá the destroyer. By some curious juxtaposition Om the Supreme was substituted for Mary, so that modern Protestant Christendom is worshiping at the shrine of a masculine trinity, while the devout Catholic still clings to Mary as the mother of his God, and supreme in her superiority over all other mothers of the race.—B.

doing, for they ascribed to their incarnation the qualities of Om, and have taught ever since that in their Jesus the world beheld the visible author of the universe itself.

They unhesitatingly ascribed to this avatar all the qualities that India and Chaldea ascribed to Brahm, adding also the office of Vishnu, and in the combination the Christian world supposes that it has in the Christ, the Om or All in all, which is the true translation of the Word.*

To the thoughtful student of Oriental metaphysical thought it seems strange that the Christian world should be so blind to the true origin of its god ideas, but the average European is not far enough advanced in the knowledge of spirit or how it is acquired to give credit to other nations for wisdom excelling his own attainments. Therefore, Europeans borrow from the older writings all that they have of spiritual wisdom, but not having a spiritual development they understand little of the meaning of their sacred writings, and attribute to the characters in them the qualities of soul that belong to their own half developed spiritual mentality.†

---

*Probably few words have ever puzzled the ignorant translators of the Sanscrit so much as this word Om, yet in the words used to designate Divinity we have Omnipotent, Omniscient, Omnipresent and Omnific, all of which the shorter Sanscrit word fully conveys to the mind of the devout worshiper as the highest conception of Divinity—the impersonal Om.

† This characteristic is still seen in the theological mentality of the Christian nations at this age. While they tenaciously cling to what little spiritual knowledge they have acquired in the past, they strenuously oppose the idea of a spiritual evolution that causes the mind to regard their creedal definitions of spirituality as im-

The Christian peoples in the age of the Cæsars could not have had a high degree of spirituality, for they were a horde of barbarians whose highest conception of power was brute force, and whose chief occupation was war. Their descendants to this day cannot understand why the people of the Oriental world have such a regard for spiritual ideas, and despise them for their deference to them, but the people of the East had their evolution from the savage plane centuries before the Western nations, and attained to some degree of knowledge concerning the spiritual life and its laws long ago, which has never been lost by them, although subjected to many extra additions by ignorance or craft.

The people of the West had their spiritual evolution in the sphere of animality and crime They were never at peace long enough to have a generation born free of the taint of blood and strife, and their religious tenets all reflect the mental bias of a people that have never conceived of the greater power of peace and benevolence toward the children of men by the Divine Creator.

They attributed to Him the same bloody disposition they bred in themselves and cried unto Him to assist them when they marched out to battle against their fellow men, when the earth ran red with the blood of the slain who worshiped at the shrine of the same embodied deity whom they felicitously describe as the Prince of Peace.

---

perfect, and remain in the atmosphere of the thought bred in the obscurity of the mediæval ages. Occasionally the creedal environment is broken by the expanding intellectual power of the imprisoned soul, but at much pain and cost to the emancipated mind.—B.

Thus has the world been mocked by the declension from the ancient doctrines which said "Thou shalt not kill;" and, as if to apologize for their violation of its most evident sanctity, the Christian world has embodied in their sacred writings that the Supreme Om delivered up to a sacrificial death the only true incarnation of the Divine Essence that ever came upon earth. This abhorrent doctrine is still taught in their temple and ghastly symbols stand before their altars that the children of future generations may be reminded at what a cost the human race could hope to obtain eternal happiness, and what a sacrifice was necessary for the redemption of the world.*

There is, indeed, a practical repudiation of this idea by a small portion of the Christian world, but they in turn are repudiated by it as not Christian but Buddhists in belief, and the highest wisdom of the Christian world in its delineation of the Divine Word ascribes to Him the nature of Siva or destroyer. To those who fail to accept the doctrines woven about their trinity, they have reserved the punishment and torture in the

* The barbaric theology of Paul and Calvin is the surviving record of the ideas in which creedal Christianity had its primitive evolution. Like the fossil footprints in the rocks, it witnesses to the existence of that savagery that made Roman civilization a power in the realm of brutal forces, but which never lifted the mind above the plane of savage ideas concerning the nature of Divinity. Even now there are sermons preached and creeds read to familiarize the mind with the sacred mystery of the atonement that savage theology attributed to the Divine Nature. Nothing is more repulsive to the Hindoo mind than the idea of a bloody sacrifice to propitiate a god, and the holding of this doctrine by the missionaries is the secret of the rejection of their other ideas by the educated Hindoos.—B.

world eternal, which savages in mortal life inflict upon the persons of their enemies taken in war.

These children of a savage race are invading India with a modification of these cruel doctrines, and are deriding the gods of the Hindoo faith as absurd creations of the fancy, but what are they bringing in place of those which they ignore or despise?

Their wisest minds are uncertain of any proof of the existence of a spiritual world, for they declare that since their god departed from earth the world of spirit has been closed against the return of any from its distant shores. Their creeds are iron bound in this respect, and they look in vain for his coming, for nearly two thousand years have departed and there is no sign of his existence given from the world of spirits that his followers may know of a surety that he still lives—a god to answer the cries of his worshipers.

The supreme power with which his believers invest him is not exercised in their behalf, and they, like the heathen world, live and die, in hope of a blessed life or in despair of any life whatever. It is their highest wisdom, and while they are self-complacently asserting the certainty of their acceptance by the Almighty Power they cling to mortal life with as much tenacity as the most illiterate savage; or, it may be said, with more fear of departure, for the savage has no fear of his god, nor does he have any idea that the eternal world is a doubtful abode for the inhabitants of earth.

The wisdom of the Divine Word in Christian nations is a sad departure from its primitive interpretation in the days of the ancient philosophy. Then Om meant the eternal and everlasting power that governed the heavens and the earth, and by whom or from whom proceeded everything that was made. He was in the beginning before the gods, and He was with the gods as well as the controlling power of the gods, and without Him was nothing made that was made.

So far the Christian faith accords with the Hindoo philosophy, but when they added "And the Word was made flesh and dwelt among us," they fabricated the wildest form of fictitious interpretation of the ancient doctrines.

The Hindoo avatarship had a very opposite meaning from this Western paraphrasing of the doctrine of the incarnation of a god, for in the Hindoo faith a god as a spirit might take the form of a man and be born upon earth, but no Hindoo ever taught that the Supreme Om descended to that state. Brahm might be embodied in Brahma; Vishnu might come to earth as Chrishna or Gautama, and Siva might show himself upon earth in the form of Mahmood or Tamerlane with a ghastly train of the slain in his wake of victory; but the Supreme Om remained in the Hindoo mind beyond the sphere of earth or its surroundings, and it is only in the barbarous conceits of the savage tribes of Christian Europe that the Ruler of the Universe was ever visible in mortal form.

That such a people should be conceited enough to claim the final destiny of the human race to be at the disposal of their god is not surprising, for they have attempted to conquer and dispose of the whole earth as their personal possessions, and such minds are ever ambitious to be rulers in the world eternal if they can obtain the requisite authority over the mentally undeveloped.

However, in reality the Supreme Om has wisely

made this impossible, and the ambitious prelates and tyrants of the European nations have a very low position in the life everlasting until they emerge from the influence of their barbarous ideas concerning the destiny of other nations. Few among them even understand that the Divine Wisdom is attained by a spiritual evolution of the mental powers, and it is a sad fact that in the spiritual world the most dense ignorance of the laws of progress prevails among the inhabitants that have received their ideas from the teachings of Christian theologians.

These latter guides of the uneducated masses are themselves unfortunate in their misconception of the meaning of the Word, and while endeavoring to expound it to their hearers, are themselves sadly in need of some one to instruct them as to its original significance. No class on earth are so incompetent as these teachers of spiritual matters, for they have lost, or rather never have had, the primitive meaning of the terms expressed to them, and most of them are under the bondage of the superstition that the original writers of their Scriptures were men to whom came a direct revelation of the Supreme Om, so little do they know of the subject of spiritual life or its effect upon the life of earth.*

* This arraignment of the teachers of Christian theology, coming from a Hindoo, must be fairly treated by the thoughtful mind. With subtle analysis of motive as well as almost supernatural acuteness of perception, he exposes the position of the mental world of Christendom as it appears to the more highly intellectual development of the East. Nor should the Christian complain of its severity, for in teaching the atonement and refusing to look into the claims of spiritual phenomona, the world of Christendom must be regarded in spirit as both cruel and ignorant by the less bigoted mind of the Oriental thinkers.—B.

I have measured quite accurately the mental power of the wise minds of the Western nations, O children of Brahm, and to you, even in your declension, they are as infants. Even in the world of spirits their great teachers come to learn of the Brahmas and Buddahs of our nation concerning the sources of planetary creation, for they as yet are not high enough in the grade to know how to make a world, and they seek our spheres that they may learn of the Brahmas how worlds are made, that they may impress their brethren yet in the flesh with the secrets of material creation.

For their wisdom is only material and their highest knowledge pertains to earthly matters. They know nothing of spirit or its power over the world of matter, and their ignorance is so dense that some of them aver that worlds and their inhabitants are built by the "fortuitous combination of atoms," which they ascribe to some unknown and unknowable power from which all proceeds that ever exists.

These children of the West are wise indeed in what they can see and measure by the physical senses, but when they enter the sphere of the vast, and to them, unknown realm of causation, they halt with uncertain feet upon the threshold, as if all of existence was to be measured and comprehended in the realm of physical being. Spirit that permeates the worlds universal is to them unknowable because in their evolution from the savage plane they have not come to the period of spiritual birth, and they cannot see causation without they attain this power in the physical or the spiritual world. Most of them never attain it in the mortal state and their wisest minds come to the life eternal as babes in spiritual truths, which they have to learn ere they can ever attain to the wisdom that pertains to creative knowledge.*

Therefore, the children of light need not look to these barbarian conquerers of the physical world for the ancient wisdom, and when they come bearing the ancient writings which once went to them from India and Persia, let them be respectfully treated by the sacred caste, but let them understand that in things spiritual they are yet children whose wisdom is that of babes, prattling about that of which they have heard, but of which they are of too immature mentality to understand.

The wisdom of the Divine Word is too deep for these Western missionaries to perceive with their present low grade of mentality. They may come with pure and self-sacrificing motives, but they know little or nothing of the nature of the Supreme Om, if they think their childish conceptions of Him are creditable to His character. He governs the universe as well as the earth, and Brahm and all the lesser gods are subject to His will, but He has given to none the disposal of the immortal natures that belong to any of His worlds. They are His, and to Him alone are they amenable. Brahmin and Sudra, Pagan and Christian, civilized or savage, all that live or ever shall live, are His children,

* This allusion to the status of material scientists is too true to be questioned. While they have the power to go into the material realm and deal with mechanical powers and even approach the chemical plane upon its material environment, they seem unable to advance to the conception of the idea of mental forces acting behind all the chemical and mechanical relations to produce the phenomena of the universal cosmos.—B.

and to them He bestows the knowledge of the Divine Word when they arrive at that stage of growth whereby they comprehend the meaning of immortal and eternal existence in their own conscious spiritual life.

## CHAPTER V.

### THE COMING OF THE BUDDHA TO ALL NATIONS.

In the ancient Vedantic writings there was originally a paragraph that has been the subject of much discussion among the Brahmin priesthood, viz.: The coming to earth of the spiritually enlightened. To the spiritually blind this Scriptural idea has always been a mystery, for to the blind there is no sensation of light or color whereby they can compare or ascertain a truth that depends upon sight, and in the province of the spiritual senses this law holds equally good as in the sphere of physical perception.

To explain this requires a familiarity with certain principles that pertain to what the material scientists of the Western nations call the law of evolution. In brief, this power of the soul of man to perceive knowledge above the plane of the physical senses depends upon a growth of mental faculties that are extremely sensitive to the finer range of power, as the eye is more sensitive than the ear or sense of touch to the lower, physical realm.

When one has the development upon the spiritual plane so that the corresponding senses which convey ideas in the physical world are capable of exercise, such a person is a Buddha or enlightened one, and if the development is very high in the powers of sensitiveness the Buddha becomes able to perceive and to teach ideas relative to the invisible world which are entirely beyond the province of the earthly senses to perceive or understand.

Because of this the tendency of the earthly disciples has been to apotheosize the Buddahs and to regard them as beings of a superior order, but the truth is that all Buddhas are only individuals of an abnormal spiritual unfoldment in the physical life; and, while they may reflect the wisdom of the life eternal, they are not gods to be worshiped or of a different nature from the rest of humanity.

The Buddhas of India have always been noted for their strong spiritual ideality, and their lives have been the subject of poetry and song to such an extent that their true mission to the world has been misunderstood and often entirely misconstrued. When a Buddha is to be born the ante-natal conditions have to be markedly positive in the development of the embryotic spirit that is to reflect the wisdom of the life eternal.

The parents are subjects of much interest to the invisible guardians of the coming life, and the mother is of special regard, for upon the mental bias of her thoughts at that period depends the greater problem of what the mind of the child shall be.

Consequently it is not entirely a myth that the great spiritual teachers of the world have had their future earthly mission foretold by angelic visitations to the mothers of the Buddhas, for nothing would or could have a greater impress upon the unfolding mind than the thought of the mother that the child was to be the charge of the inhabitants of the world invisible and reveal its mysteries to the children of earth.

When it is recorded in the traditions of the nation that the Buddhas are conceived by rays of light from the heavens, it is only a poetic expression of the mental bias of the recipient of heavenly wisdom, for the mind of a Buddha is shaped and moulded by influences from the world of spirits, and the mission of the Buddhas is to teach the truth concerning the spiritual world in the language of the people to whom they come as inspired messengers of truth.

They are not incarnations of developed spirits, who have once lived upon the earth as men, nor are they spirits from other planets undergoing a new experience in the sphere of earth, but they are able to reflect the wisdom of such spirits, for their mental powers are more susceptible to the influence of the higher life than that of earth, and they easily converse with spiritual intelligences of a very high degree of spiritual unfoldment.

This gives them the credit and appearance of being supernaturally endowed with wisdom, and has been the basis of a mischievous error in the theology of India, for the appearance of a Buddha, according to the perverted construction of the ancient doctrines, is the signal for the apotheosizing of another person as a god, thus adding another to the long list of decarnated spirits who are worshiped as having more power in the eternal world than their position there entitles them to possess.

For in the life of spirit the Buddhas, however great they may have been upon earth, are only parts of a system that has for its object the general diffusion of spiritual light to the world of mortals. When their work is done upon earth they pass to their proper place in the life eternal, and the cries of their deluded but sincere followers for personal favors cannot be answered except upon general principles.

The Buddhas of the world are the torch bearers of the world of spirit, and while they enlighten the earth with the knowledge of spiritual life and its laws, they do not make that life, nor can they control the destiny of the souls who enter it from any nation or sphere of earth. Therefore, to regard them as saviors in any such sense as the Christian world teaches is to place them in a false position in the spiritual world and retards the minds upon earth from receiving that light of the spirit, which would make the work of the Buddhas of immense value to mortals.

India has had her generations who have rejoiced in the light of spiritual revelation from the Buddhas, but she has forgotten that the Buddhistic light was to shine upon all souls throughout the earth, according to the ancient doctrines, and when her priests suppressed this cardinal truth they went into that twilight darkness of mind whereby the pure light of the ancient Vedas was nearly obscured.

In place of the brilliant illumination of the mind from the light of the highest heavens, the mental powers grew feeble, and instead of a recognition of the true principle whereby the real truth is to be ascertained, a false system of ascetic mortification of the flesh was adopted, and spiritual darkness, instead of radiant power, invested the Brahmin priesthood until Gautama appeared, the last of the greater Buddhas that has ever arisen in India since the age of Capilya.

Gautama taught the greater truths of the ancient faiths, but he did not assail the errors as a soul of more positive intellect would have done. He should have revealed the ancient faith in greater power, and would have done so had he taught the original interpretation of the doctrines of reincarnation and transmigration of the spirit from sphere to sphere after it had left the sphere of earth. From the failure to do this, and because India lies helpless at the feet of Caste, the spiritual power of her people has fallen so low that the shrines of millions of earth bound spirits are receiving the homage due the great Om, and from those shrines not even the ancient wisdom is reflected from the world of spirits, but a crude mass of superstitious decrees that are conceived in ignorance and gestated and born in craft.

Well does this condition exemplify the ancient prophecy, that when the Buddhas cease to come the people shall sink in spiritual knowledge, and also does it prove true that each age, and even generation, should have its Buddha if the world would not lose its regard for the life eternal.

For the Buddhahood is not attained by the mere belief in its existence. India has had its principles taught for centuries, but its light comes not as in the days of Sakya, nor do the priesthood of Benares or the rest of the nation dwell in that spiritual freedom that belongs to the spiritually illuminated. They, like the Christian priests of the West, are in only a reflected light from the written Word, but the transcendent glory of a spiritual revelation of the eternal life is not shining upon them, as it should and would, were they free from the superstition of caste and dogma.

There would be no cloud of ignorance and doubt to hang above the sacred altars, were the ministrants at the altars as pure in their inner lives as their external garments symbolize, for the power of the spirit comes to those only who are pure in spirit, and the Buddhahood is given to such freely.

Therefore, it comes to those of any nation or people who seek its influence, but it comes not in the pride of caste or glory of earthly grandeur.

Gautama obtained it by self-renunciation, and all souls who would have its pure light must live in its presence as though they stood in the sphere of Brahm, to whom the darkness and the light are the same. The sons of Brahm who seek the Buddhahood should not seek it in the spirit of pride or self-will. It is a sacred gift of the spiritual world, and in that world the spirit of the suppliant is the index of the power that is to be given.

The Buddhas who teach are specially gifted by birth and spiritual instruction from the womb, but the Buddhas who are taught do not always receive this experience, although they can obtain all its real benefits in their own lives, and become fitted thereby to obtain a blessed entrance into the Nirvanian heavens.

## CHAPTER VI.

### THE COMING OF THE MISSIONARIES FROM THE WESTERN NATIONS.

It has ever been taught in some of the Vedantic traditions that the time would come when the Buddha light should come to the world again—not from India, but from the Western world that sat in darkness and the valley of the shadow of death.

Compared with the spiritual light that anciently shone over India's plains, that of Europe is of the crudest character, for her greatest minds were never able to perceive the universality of spirit, and they are yet in the spiritual darkness that belongs to the first stages of a spiritual unfoldment.

Still the teachers of those nations have been able to sense the pulsations of the great spiritual force that governs the universe, and in their crude conceptions of its power have supposed that they have perceived all of its principles, and have adopted in essence the conclusions of the ancient Indian faith, viz.. that the supreme Brahm has had one incarnation.

How the Supreme could become a mortal they have never tried to explain, but some of their priests have written in their sacred books that it was so, and upon that basis the present religious worship of the Western nations is established. In reality, this theory of the incarnation of the Supreme is but a transfer of the Indian avatarship, or the coming to earth of Vishnu as a spiritual force, but such is the ignorance of the

Christian world regarding the religious ideas of other nations that it imagines itself to be the chosen channel of all the spiritual light that has ever come to earth. It was in consequence of this ignorance that the people of the West pushed out their missions to the so-called heathen nations, and had their wisdom been in any degree equal to their zeal, they might have done a great work of good to the nations of the East, but the Christian world made the mistake of copying the errors as well as the truths of the systems from which their faith was taken, and in so doing became shorn of that power for good which their efforts deserved.

They found that the East, from which they borrowed all the spiritual light they ever have had, understood better than themselves the origin of the doctrines and they have only succeeded to a limited degree in attracting attention to their work.

The Christian missionary has ever had an invisible but powerful foe to contend with in his work in India. The mighty hosts of India that have been and are still linked with the mental atmosphere of earth, through a misunderstanding of the doctrine of reincarnation, have ever been exerting a silent, but positive, influence upon the minds of the natives against the reception of the Christian theories of spirit, and they have wisely done this, for the Christian theories are in the main erroneous in nearly all essential points regarding the nature of the soul and its destiny. To change the superstitions of Hindooism for the equally superstitious theories of Christianity would do no good, and until the superstitions of both are discarded India cannot rise very high in the scale of spiritual unfoldment.

The Christian missionary has his work to do in India, but it is not to convert the people of that country to his theories of religion. He is sent there and sustained by a certain grade of spiritual power, but it is rather that the observer of spiritual powers may perceive that behind all the religious systems of earth is a universal principle that works out through all nations the same essential results, and that each nation reflects to some degree the wisdom and beneficence of the Almighty purpose in human existence. For the nations of the West are but the children of the East in spiritual knowledge and their religious ideas are the fruit of the wisdom of the Eastern world transferred to new conditions that it may have a new expression in the process of a new mental evolution of the race.

The Western nations were never spiritual in their primal life. Egypt, the mother of their civilization, was crude and material in her conceptions of immortal existence. Greece and Rome were never able to go very high in the grade of a spiritual unfoldment, although Greece, through her philosophy, imparted some of the wisdom she received from the Oriental world. Rome was material and cruel, but while her mission was to subdue the barbarian hordes of Europe, she never rose above the grade of material force in her concepts of a spiritual life. When her temporal power was withdrawn from the surrounding nations she sought supremacy by cultivating the superstitious nature of the people, and through that channel sought to maintain her jurisdiction over the nations of the West. But her spiritual power was supported by the ignorant and crafty in the spiritual world and her rule upon earth was bloody and deceitful.

The highest light she ever could attain was by the

lurid flames of persecution, and her mental vision peopled the world eternal with the hosts of the devils damned, over whom the Siva of the Indian trinity reigned supreme. There was no light in her creed, and she has never been able to perceive the senseless folly of supposing that the Supreme Om would ever intrust to such incompetent hands the work of enlightening a world as to the nature of its origin or a knowledge of its destiny.

Rome, the parent of modern Christianity, is the harlot of the spiritual world. She debases and degrades all that pertains to the subject, and from her seat upon the seven hills pollutes the fountains of spiritual truth with deliberate design.

From the time when her ancient priests perverted the great truths that came from India, through the missions of the disciples of Gautama, Rome has been the deliberate thief of ideas and the dispenser of fabrications concerning the spiritual world. She is the source from which the Western world take their embodied thought, and she is the only earthly channel through which any knowledge was allowed to reach the Western nations for a thousand years.

All the writings that belonged to the sacred classics were under her manipulation, and the Western nations were fed upon spiritual falsehood as truth, until they knew not whether the foundation of their faith was laid in truth or upon a substructure of fabrication. Her priests were cunning and subtle, but their work was false, and were it not for the eternal nature of truth, and the ability of the lovers of truth in the world of spirits to reach earth through the Buddhahood, the

Western world would remain in spiritual darkness for countless generations.

Even as it is, the work of enlightenment will be tedious, for the minds of the West have been so long fed upon spiritual error and falsehood that the truth is distasteful to most of them, and they reject it when presented.

It is not because they prefer darkness to light, but because in their mental growth they have been debarred from a perception of spiritual knowledge, and in their ignorance they blindly follow the leadership of their blind guides to that extent that neither of them reach the pathway that leads to spiritual wisdom. Such is the spiritual leadership of the Romish form of the Christian theory of a spiritual life; and now we turn to the Protestant form of the faith to see what that presents for India to accept.

Protestant Christians have the foundation of their faith in the same traditions of the avatarship as their Romish progenitors. On that question they are equally agreed and equally in error. They broaden the field of Christian effort, but have no provision for those that are unfortunate enough to doubt the truth of their dogmas. They, too, limit the goodness and power of the Supreme Om to provide for the myriads whose spiritual existence is as much a necessity as their own, and ascribe to the governor of the universe the malignity of a fiend toward those who reject the doctrines that are recorded in the books; consequently, the Protestant world of Christianity is, and must be, bound by the limits their theologians have devised, and cannot rise to that conception of the universal power that provides for all created life. It is narrow and will remain so until the intellectual power of its believers is developed to that degree that enables them to perceive the Supreme Om has made provision for all the children of men in his majestic benevolence and almighty power.

The missionaries of the Western world have not as yet arisen to this recognition of the Creator of the Universe. What, then, have they to offer to India that India has not already obtained in the province of spiritual thought. The answer is this: India had ignored the principles of the ancient faith, and her people were going down into spiritual darkness. The barbarian minds of the West had taken a modified degree of the light which India had transmitted to the West, and by its return the people, who were losing their knowledge and faith in the power of spiritual enlightenment, were thus reminded that all nations had an inheritance in the life eternal. The Western missionaries brought back the light that Gautama had transmitted to them, and the Vedantic prophecy, that light should come from the West, had its first fulfillment in the coming of the missionaries who supposed they were bringing to the East a knowledge of life and immortality.

The missionary knew nothing of the real power that inspired him to this work, but with blind zeal he set out upon his mission and in honest ignorance thought he was led by the Spirit of his God to preach the truth to a people who were dwelling in dense spiritual darkness.

He was often met with great opposition, but not from any other motive than disregard for his ignorance of Indian thought. He has made no serious inroads as yet upon Hindoo superstitions, and will not, for they are to be dispelled by the influx of light from the Hindoo heavens rather than the Christian, as the latter is of too doubtful a character to bestow much illumination upon the inhabitants of their own lands, whereas to the Hindoo world in spirit is delegated the task of enlightening the world of both spirits and mortal with the knowledge of spiritual life in all its gradations.

For the Christian world is not spiritual, but material, and its ideas of the life eternal are nearly all erroneous. It thinks itself the favored recipient of spiritual revelation, yet had it not appropriated the spiritual doctrines of the Oriental world, it would have been entirely destitute of any revelation whatever. The people of the Western nations were never high enough in the scale of mental unfoldment to have a clear idea of the source of spiritual revelation, and, save a limited number, have no perception of the real truth concerning their own doctrines. They cannot discern spiritual ideas for they have no spiritual insight; and, although they can feel the influx of spiritual power, they know not its source and blindly follow it in a superstitious manner or reject it altogether. Therefore, India has nothing to hope for from them and their missionaries, for with the good they bring they also fail to understand that they are spiritually blind and the Supreme Om has not favored them more than others with a true revelation.

In fact, the Western nations are just coming to a knowledge of the existence of a spiritual birth, which was taught in India ages ago. It comes to them with the vivid reality of a revelation, but the priesthood of the West is so ignorant of its source that they have banded themselves to oppose it, and, if possible, prevent the people from being influenced by it. They cannot control this power, therefore they oppose it; but it will spread in spite of their antagonism, and in time will serve to illumine its people with a knowledge of spirituality free from the superstitious ideas that now are a portion of its dogmas.

The missions of the Western world to India are a part of a great spiritual movement to familiarize the people of earth with each others ignorance of the principles of eternal life. No religion that holds sway on earth has any intrinsic merit of its own, and all of them are reflections of the more or less crude mentality of the different races or tribes. Most of the formulated systems are the work of ignorance and craft, and while they serve their purpose as a power to keep the minds of people from utterly forgetting the ideas of spiritual life, they have little influence in determining the status of the soul in that life.

The most ascetic Brahmin may imagine himself to be of more importance than his Buddhist or Christian neighbor, but when he touches the shores of the eternal world he will find his asceticism or caste is a barrier or obstacle to that spirit of fraternization which belongs to the higher spiritual development, and many of them will be compelled to wander among the spirits of the earth bound, where caste is recognized as a controlling power.

The Christian priest who teaches that only those who accept his god can be saved will have for his companions those who teach a smmilar creed, but the vast host of intelligent and philosophic souls who have lived above the power of creed will let the Christian heavens fight out their battles of thought without participating in the bloodless strife. Those who prefer to cling to the blood stained altars of Kali* will enter the kingdom of savage spirits who have not yet outgrown the primitive worship of ancestral ignorance, and those who have mistaken the symbols of the phallus for objects of worship will have the spirits of bulls and swine for companions in the world eternal, until they learn that the life of the soul is not to be wasted in brutal sensuality.

India went into spiritual darkness when she took the images for objects of divine worship, and the missionaries are doing a good work when they point to the results of idolatrous worship, for if the imagery is not explained to the mind it becomes an obstacle to the perfect understanding of the idea represented by it.

The linga and the phallus were originally the symbols of the source of visible life, but they were not designed to be objects of worship or to excite the lustful passions. The triple deities were designed to represent the equality of all the powers of nature, viz.: Creation, preservation and destruction, or birth, life and death; but they were not images of embodied deities in the original symbols, although in after ages they were worshiped as such.

The lesser deities that were taught as having jurisdiction over mortals were but the disembodied spirits of the savage and barbarous tribes who sought through

*Kali is one of the ancient goddesses of India, who is still worshiped with blood sacrifices. She belongs to the most ancient cult, and is represented as a black female. Probably she is a survivor of the transition of the worship, from offering human sacrifices to the substitution of animals in their place.

the power of spirit return to preserve their power upon earth by worship, but they had no real power in the world of spirits to become gods or to control the affairs of men.

Often have the wise men of India warned its people that their deities were powerless to help them, and that not Brahm, but Om, was to be the object of their homage; but the warning was not heeded, and India has sunk in power, both of body and mind, as she prostrates herself before the spiritual gods of the lesser grades.

The Western nations that overthrew the worship of their old gods of the lesser rank and embodied their worship in one form were wiser in this than if they had clung to the worship of the lesser spirits, for they released the latter from their hold upon the earth and at the same time broke the chains which bind souls to earth who wish to be worshiped there as heroes or gods.* Therefore, although the missionaries have invaded India with their crude god, or another form of the Buddhist worship, they have brought with them a powerful body of spirits who have entered the shrines of the ancient temples and are releasing the earth bound spirits there from their hold upon the altars and teaching them that the pathway to a state of spiritual blessedness is not in seeking worship, but in escaping from it.

*This is a most singular statement of the effect of concentrating the minds of people upon any one as a god. If it be true no greater misfortune can befall a spirit than to have fame or attention from the minds of people on earth. What a hopeless sense of helplessness a mind must have that is the center of the thought of millions, yet unable to transcend the laws of individual soul development, no matter how intense the agony of the suppliant.—B.

The missionaries will not convert mortals so much as release spirits, and while from the world of spirits we would reach the priesthood with the truth about the Christian dogmas, at the same time we would say that it is not wise to continue to worship the spirits as gods nor to call upon them to aid in a work that properly belongs to the soul to do for itself.

Further than this there is no more sacred revelation from the world of spirit to be made to either Brahmin or Christian. There will be plenty of spiritual revelations, but not for the purpose of confirming the superstitions that have arisen since the days of the ancient teachers. You may expect that the gods that speak now will explain the past and instruct for the future, but the day for the claim of revelation from the Supreme Om is past, save as he reveals through the process of natural law.

Thus, O sons of Brahm, should you answer the teachers of the Western world: "We know your gods for we gave them to you. We know how the voice of the Supreme speaks, for we heard his words and gave them to you. We know who your angels and spirits are for we had them long ere you knew of them, and while they may be gods to you they are no longer to be called gods by us. You have come to us as bearers of good tidings, for which we give you thanks; but we sent the ideas to you first, and if the message does you good we know that it is the same for you as for all nations.

"But we also know that you received it from us, and if Om has spoken to us as well as you, boast not as if you had more than we. Learn what India has to teach in all her symbols ere you judge her harshly, and look well that she who long ago taught of the soul cannot teach you much of the spiritual life of which as yet you know nothing."

Thus answer the teachers of the West in wisdom, O sons of Brahm.

## CHAPTER VII.

### THE INFLUX OF ORIENTAL IDEAS AMONG THE WESTERN NATIONS.

Scarcely had the missions of the West been established throughout the East than there came to the people of Europe and America a strange manifestation of power from the world of spirit. It was heralded by no prophetic order, and it utterly refused to obey or affiliate with the religious ideas that had become so firmly fastened upon the mind of the Christian nations that they were esteemed to be the only religious ideas based upon truth.

The Christian world at first received the phenomena with incredulity and wonder, but as time elapsed began to regard it with undisguised hostility and open antagonism. The reason of this treatment of a great phenomenal fact was that the intelligence that came from the spiritual world refused to indorse the theories of the Christian priesthood as spiritual truth, and the latter soon placed themselves in battle array against any attempt to further enlighten the world through such a source.

In taking this course, the Christian priesthood only followed the process whereby the priests of all religions seek to preserve their power; for the priests of the religious systems are the spiritual tyrants of the world, or if pure motives govern them, the natural born instructors of things pertaining to the spiritual nature.

In the Western nations the spiritual evolution of its

tribes was much retarded by the primitive savagery and bloody barbarism of the people. Europe especially was far behind the Oriental world in its spiritual growth, and its people were incapable of comprehension of spiritual truth for many centuries previous to the Christian era, and were in gross darkness for subsequent generations. Its priesthood was ignorant and degraded; it was incapable of comprehending or teaching the subtle principles of the spiritual life, and a crude jargon of ideas regarding the life of this world and the other filled the minds of both priest and people. The writings that their chief teachers had stolen or copied from the Oriental world were pronounced to be of Divine origin, and millions of spirits went from earth to the spirit world firmly believing that they alone had an inheritance in the life eternal, from which all other people were to be excluded.

The practical effect of this dogma upon the mortals of the Christian nations was to impress them with inordinate pride and vanity, and they taught and firmly believed that to them only had come any revelation of the true nature of life and all other nations were subjects of the vindictive wrath of the Almighty.

Such being the status of Christian dogma, there arose a purpose of better instruction concerning the life of the spirit among the sages of the so-called heathen world, and they first instructed some of the more intelligent European and American spirits in the principles that govern spiritual and material relations, whereby the latter were able to introduce to the people of their countries the spiritual phenomena that had been for ages a familiar subject of Oriental observation. The people of the West thought it at first a system of spiritual revelation that could be utilized for material advantages, and have valued it or discarded it proportionate to its availability in the accumulation of material wealth.

With the short-sightedness of their ignorant disregard of principle, many of their leaders of thought have been secret believers in the new ideas and at the same time open opponents of their propagation, on the ground that the people were not ready for the truth and had better be left to work on in the old error until they had ascertained the truth by personal experience.

These Christian prelates who so violently oppose the possible admission of the spiritual world to a recognition as a sentient reality forget that their whole system had its foundation in similar phenomena, and in their blind zeal to exclude the light from the world are deliberately closing the avenues of the mind from receiving the only knowledge of a spiritual kind that is worth obtaining, and thereby hold the mental powers upon the old plane of fabulous tradition or crafty fabrication.

Such is the true status of the Christian theologians of this age. They have filled the world of mortals with the most absurd tales about the Divine Nature and its attributes, for they have no perception of the source of their dogmas. They have filled the heavens of Europe with myriads of earth bound souls who cannot rise above the idea that they are the only saved people in existence, yet whose mentality is so low that they cannot understand the first idea of spiritual progress, or by what steps they can free themselves from the passions and influence of earth.

In the influx from the Oriental world the first measures necessary were to emancipate the Western mind from the slavish fear or regard for the priestly orders. Consequently the mind of the thinkers became of a skeptical turn, and the first result of their liberty was iconoclastic zeal in destroying the barriers to mental progress that craft and superstition had erected. Many of the most talented minds of the West were termed infidel by their Christian neighbors, not because they were false to any principle, but because they were too intelligent to be imposed upon by the fabrications of the Christian priesthood.

The latter raged and cursed in vain, for they no longer had the support of the physical power through the civil law to enforce their bloody edicts against the growth of mind, which has always been deemed heretical, and the infidel, or rather the intelligent mind of the West has made far more progress in mental and spiritual evolution than their superstitious traducers.

Now, it is a principle in the relations of spiritual and mortal life that the mentality in either world follows in parallel lines, and that the progress of one mind from one plane to another affects all souls upon either plane, so that when a person gets a new idea his expression of it either in language or thought sets a current of mental force in motion that extends to every soul or spirit within the radius of its sphere of influence. Hence, when the Oriental world in spirit began to send its thoughts upon the Western nations, the souls in sympathy with the ideality taught, caught up the thoughts and sent them reverberating through both the spiritual and mortal worlds.

The Christian world in both spiritual and mortal conditions felt the shock most, for it had such an inferior growth of spiritual perception that it supposed itself to be the most intelligent in spiritual knowledge of all, not even knowing its own ignorance. Hence, in its ignorance it opposed the influx of light, both in spirit and mortal life, and while its inhabitants of the spirit world are using the natural laws governing the two conditions, they carefully conceal from their mortal compatriots their true nature, and the latter, feeling their influence, suppose it to be the direct influx of the Holy Spirit, or the third person of their Trinity.

Those who have ever attended the places of Christian worship, where the devotees work themselves up to a great pitch of excitement* in calling upon their god, will notice the similarity of their emotions to those of the dervishees, who, in their ecstacy of excitement, suppose themselves to be in the direct embrace of their god; and, in fact, the same cause lies at the foundation of the phenomena in each, viz.. ignorance of the laws of spiritual influx that opens the mind to sensations above the plane of the physical sense merely.

The opening of the doors of the world of spirit to the people of the Western nations was the signal of an irruption of the vast hord of ignorant and crude spiritual beings that had been sent from these nations into

* This explanation of the revival influence that attends the labors of many Christian teachers accords perfectly with the Oriental doctrine of thought transference upon the different planes of spirit. The mentality of the soul upon any plane always responds to any influence that belongs to that plane, and as the Christian planes of thought vary, the various sects naturally correspond with the different grades. Philosophic minds do not regard the exhibition of mental excitement as of any great importance or evidence of any operation of the supernatural order, as do the ignorant.—B.

the spirit world before they had had time to outgrow the errors of their earthly lives, and the advent of their return to earth was soon seen in the gross ignorance and contradictory statements made by them relative to the life in the world of spirits.

Especially was this observed among the believers in the deity of their incarnated god, for the inhabitants of the Christian world of Europe were in such a chaotic realm of intellectual thought that they failed lamentably in realization of their hopes of a future life. Their Savior was not, as they had been taught, the ruler of the world eternal, and aside from a band of ambitious prelates, who had arranged spectacular representations of their god, there was nothing existent in the world of spirits that corresponded with their religious ideas of earth.

They sought in vain for that embodied representative of the Almighty, which they had so boastingly paraded before the people of other nations as their god, and the only god ever incarnate, but they found that personality of gods has no recognition in spiritual life, and that individual development only was the criterion of spiritual judgment.

The spirit inhabitants of the nations of the West were intellectually paralyzed by this discovery, and struggled for centuries to realize its meaning, often reverting to the mental atmosphere of earth, and there fortifying themselves anew by contact with their ignorant earthly brethren, who in turn, feeling the influx of a spiritual power they could not understand, supposed that they had a spiritual recognition from their god, and that in this manner he was fulfilling the promises recorded in their sacred books. Thus, from generation to generation, the people of the Christian world have deluded themselves with the fallacious hope that they alone have a knowledge of spiritual life and general jurisdiction over the eternal world.

It will be observed by critical students of the Christian religion that it is based upon a claim of delegated authority from the Supreme Om, and that their incarnate god transferred this authority to visible representatives, who have power to control the nations of the earth and dictate what shall be taught as truth, and what shall be prohibited.*

This claim of supreme authority has been exercised to neutralize, as far as possible, the revelations of truth from the spiritual world that transcend or explain the dogmas of the Christian religion, and intercourse with the world of spirits has been forbidden by the Christian priesthood of all denominations, not because such intercourse is impossible, but because it reveals the false foundations upon which all religions rest, viz.: ignorance of the true relations between the two conditions of life.

In a substitution of truth for the errors of religions there can be no priesthood having any authority to dictate what is or is not to be taught as spiritual truth; for, as the spiritual life is an evolution from the physical life, its progressive unfoldment will give different revelations from age to age, so that the priesthood of

* This peculiarity of the Christian system is not entirely confined to it, as there are similar sentiments held by some other great religions. It probably can be traced to the mentality awakened to the realization of the existence of a spiritual world, but not fully cognizant of the principles dominant there. Especially is this the case where the worship of some great teacher of spiritual ideas as a god prevails. Even the followers of Brahma and Buddha in this age are tinctured with it.—B.

one generation, or their ideas, cannot be authority for those of succeeding ages.* Those priests or those ideas that belong to a forgotton-past will be outgrown if the people of earth do not seek to perpetuate them by a rigid repression of the growing intellectual life of childhood, and it is here that the priesthoods of earth have exerted their power to the detriment of the race. They have held the mind of the people upon the plane of a childish regard for themselves as the chosen representatives of the Almighty Power, and in doing so have prevented that growth of intellectual vigor that belongs to spirituality of a high order, and the minds of both priest and people have been retarded in their spiritual development. India and Europe both show this to a marked degree, for each has in its spiritual literature numberless superstitions that degrade and dwarf the intellect as well as betoken a mind of childish ignorance.

When the Oriental world of spirit first sent its power into the Christian heavens, the darkness was so dense there that anything like an intelligent communication between the two spiritual spheres was entirely unknown, for, the Christian world in spirit was powerless to do more than send an influence, which its correlative on earth supposed emanated from the Supreme Spirit. It was in vain that their philosophers tried to reach the world of mortals, for Christian superstition supposed that all intercourse of an intelligible character

*One is often struck with the sublime egotism that seems to be a part and parcel of the priestly character in all nations. Standing as they do, the visible representatives of the Supreme Power, the very thought of their office seems to impregnate the mentality of the individual, and he can hardly help developing the traits of his God idea.

was Satanic, and even to this day their chief teachers so regard it It was only when the advanced philosophic minds in spirit had learned how to use the powers of nature aright that intellectual spirituality dawned upon the Western nations, and a little light was sent upon that self-conceited and spiritually blinded people.*

Like other nations, some were either dazzled by its illuminating power or blinded by its effulgence, and straightway tried to establish a priestly hierarchy over its recipients, but so far in vain.

This source of spiritual power owes nothing to earth and cares nothing for its childish expedients to control or formulate it into a series of doctrines. Mortals may seek to perpetuate a knowledge of spiritual truth through the old channels, but the world of spirit can open new avenues at will, and its present work is to dispel the darkness in which ancient superstitions are bred—not to originate a new series to curse the children of earth. Therefore, the ardent apostles of the new revelation need not think that it will be retarded by opposition or seriously benefited by their indorsement. It stands upon a different basis than the old religious systems, and while it explains them, has nothing in common with them as far as instituting creedal fetters for the soul.

The Christian world has arrayed itself in open hostility, through its priesthood, to the influx of light from

* The theories put forth by some of the writers upon the nature of the soul show this same trait, even to this day; for the moment the question arises as to the inception of soul life, the only answer is a repetition of the Oriental idea, that the spirit comes from God and returns to God in the ages of existence after death. That it holds a self-conscious eternity of progressive life unfoldment has been ignored by many teachers of both Oriental and Christian schools of thought.—B.

the spiritual world, and must take the consequences of such a foolish antagonism. Its priesthood are of all men the most to be pitied rather than censured, for they are so densely ignorant of spiritual thought outside of their spurious creeds as not to be held accountable for their childish ideas about the nature of the soul or the destiny of the spirit.*

I have alluded to their ignorance of the basic ideas of their own religion, and the tenacity with which they cling to the fabulous origin of their God-man. They little realize that not a distinguishing feature of their system is original, but even their gods are the reconstructed myths of India and Egypt. Their Trinity is a travesty upon the Hindoo Triad with Om in place of Siva, whom (Siva) they regard as the adversary of life and wisdom. Their scriptures are the stolen writings of the sages of the Oriental world, and their sacred oracles the treasured wisdom of those persons who were spiritually developed enough to have more or less intercourse with the lower spheres of the spiritual world. Of these they have made their gods, and without these they would be still worshiping at the shrines of Thor and Odin, or in the bloody rites of the Druids and the cruel deities of the nations bordering the Mediterranean. For these nations of the West were savage devotees of Moloch and Baal long after the altars of India were

*The Christian priesthood are not alone to be censured for their ignorance of the spiritual nature. Even some of the theosophical schools of India are teaching the annihilation of the spiritual entity as a possibility, where by successive rebirths the soul cannot attain a good Karma. Those who imagine that conscious life can be annihilated, once having had its inception through planetary relations, little know of the eternal relation of the universal powers of life.

purged of human sacrifice, and the remains of that bloody worship are seen in the sacrificial oblation which the Christian world believes was the culmination of Deific wrath and vengeance. To the intelligent observer such ideas have their true origin in the crude superstitions of savages, but these Western nations still teach it as the final resource of Deific wisdom to redeem a world, and it is no wonder that from the life eternal the first information that ever came in this modern age refuted such a monstrous libel upon the Divine Beneficence.

The believers in such ideas are necessarily tinctured with savagery, and their greatest glory is to rule or destroy. Hence the Christian world of mortals is devoted to war and conquest, nor do they value justice and truth except as they can dispense both; for their god, Jehovah, is, like themselves, arbitrary and bloody, remorseless and cruel to those who refuse to obey his behests. The introduction of ideas from the world of spirits denounced these crimes as worthy of judgment, and declared them to be no less than murder and falsehood. The conquest of the weak by the powerful was stigmatized as robbery, and the brutal treatment of the defenseless by the conqueror the evidence of a savage and barbarous disposition that stamped its possessor with the stigma of disgrace.

India has had her full share of the practical results of European Christianity, and when her people seek a new faith it will not be one that needs the moral support of sword and cannon to commend it to her people.

There is a land where the people of a professed Christian name have had an evolution that is more in harmony with spiritual ideas as they actually exist in the life of spirit. That land has no outward symbol of priest or king, and its people stand on an equality before the laws. To this people came the spiritual revelations of this age, and there are such exhibitions of spiritual power in all its phases as have not been recorded since the time when the Vedantic writings were given.

This people are the Buddhists of the Christian name, but they draw their best religious ideas from all lands and all peoples. Over that land has descended the spiritual aura like a silvery cloud of light, and the ancient glory of India is enveloping its nobler minds with celestial radiance. She is the friend of the oppressed of all nations, and to her let India appeal when the time comes for the return of the celestial messenger that shall bring again her ancient glory, according to the Vedantic prophecies.

## CHAPTER VIII.

### THE TRUE HISTORY OF THE CHRISTIANS' GOD.

To the students of the Indian-Scriptures there has always been a different interpretation of the symbols than that given by the scholarship of the West, and because of the ignorance of the latter the true history or even appreciation of Indian thought is an inscrutable mystery to the European mind. India long ago perceived the essential unity of life, and all her great teachers based their doctrines upon its sacred inviolability. It was taught in India before the Grecian sages came to learn of the soul, that the spiritual nature was eternal, and that change of condition did not annihilate the life principle. Upon this foundation Indian philosophy rested, and all the various sects that have arisen have never disputed its essential truth. The Brahmins, by virtue of their superior wisdom, were the first to formulate a theological system of social privilege and became the exponents of the religious ideas that they desired the people to receive, but the Brahmin caste, as a class, never was able to attain that profound spiritual knowledge that can only be obtained by those who have attained the Buddha state, and their expositions of spirituality fell far below the higher grades of Divine enlightenment.

The followers of Brahm became the observants of form, rather than possessors of spiritual power through a worthy motive, but lost rather than gained spirituality; for to be spiritual, requires not only the subordination of the flesh to the spirit but the evolution of the spirit itself, which may or may not take place parallel with the period of physical life.

When the principles of the Brahmins were carried to the West by the ancestor of the Israelites the system of caste was transferred also, and upon the shores of the Western sea a nation was formed that held some of the doctrines of the East in its religious system, but they had been more or less corrupted by the admixture of the religions of the surrounding nations.

Notably among these doctines was a perverted interpretation of the avatarship of India, which the learned priests of that country had changed into an earthly monarch who should "rule the nations with a rod of iron and dash them in pieces as a potter's vessel," while the favored disciples of the true religion would be the rulers of the other nations of the earth.

All these Messianic prophecies had long before been recorded in essence by the spiritual teachers of India, and they originally meant, that when the earth needed a spiritual teacher who should be able to teach the truth, such a teacher should come who would be able to discern and proclaim the ideas that governed the spiritual world; for as the eternal life was a sequence of the earthly, so its power could be made to appear upon earth to instruct the people there as to their destiny.

But these ideas came to people familiar with material power who never had a spiritual evolution, and who depended upon tradition for their authority. Thus the people of that nation were ever looking for the leadership of a material character, and oblivious of the spiritual meaning underlying their sacred books and symbolism.

This people, however, had some of the most ancient

writings of the Oriental world, and they treasured them with much reverence, although they did not comprehend their spiritual meaning, but there were some minds that were never quite satisfied with the interpretation of the symbolism or the traditional rendering of the writings themselves.

Among these was a man named Joschu, or Joshua, who was quite a teacher of the mystic symbolism upon a new basis, and he, being familiar with the true life of the spirit, declared that the priests and scribes of the law were ignorantly giving the people a false interpretation. So strenuous was he as to their inability to interpret the writings, that he aroused their wrath, which finally culminated in his death at their hands.

This was not the only one who had met violence at the hands of the priesthood, for so ignorant were the hereditary rulers of the nation of the law of the spirit, that they supposed it to be impossible for any revelation to be made that did not come through their order, and the appearance of a teacher of spiritual truths outside of their ranks was the signal for accusation of blasphemy against their god.

Joshua, having been duly charged with this offense, was summarily executed by being stoned to death, but his words had made some impression upon some illiterate and obscure disciples, to whom he afterward appeared from the world of spirits to confirm them in his faith, and for at least three generations he was able to make his presence felt at some of their assemblies.

To these ignorant followers the return of a spirit in a visible form, or by other means, was hailed as an evidence of Divine power, and in their traditions they ascribed to him the honor of having triumphed over death and achieved a victory that demonstrated him to be the traditional Messiah.

In reality Joshua had only done what the sages of India had long before declared to be a commonplace manifestation of the spiritual world, but to the barbarous savages of the West it seemed to be much greater, and it was not long ere they began to worship him as a god, and to formulate a system of religion with some of his sayings for doctrines.

There was another element that had much to do with shaping the religious thought of the barbarian West about the same time that Joshua was disputing with the Jewish hierarchy, viz.: the introduction of Buddhism, through the followers of Sakya -Muni, who had gone from India to the West, as well as to the nations nearer home.

These missionaries of the gospel of peace were warmly welcomed by the sages of the schools of learning in Greece and Egypt, and numbered many disciples among the learned and wise of those nations. In fact, so powerful did they become that the worship of the native deities of those countries began to decline, so that the priesthood, fearing a total overthrow of their power, set about devising measures to change the current in their own favor, and, as a consequence, the admixture of theory and truth that belonged to the systems of the followers of Joshua and also of Sakya was adopted and became the central religion of that people.

The Western priesthood did not like to attribute their worship to a teacher so far away as India, but they took Joshua and changed his name to correspond with a Greek and Latin term signifying "The One Eternal Being," and thus labeled, the Christian world has been worshiping, for centuries, a fictitious god manufactured from the legends and myths of all the religions of precedent generations, supplemented by a combination of the ideas of two religious teachers, who both were directly indebted to the spirit world for what truth they knew about the world eternal.

It is not strange that the Christian world rejects the truth of spiritual revelation in this age when it flashes so much light upon the obscurity of its origin. It was the policy of the early Christian fathers to evade the truth or conceal it under a cloud of specious pretenses, for many knew their faith was but a fabrication from the outset Nor have they ever been willing to acknowledge their duplicity in the world of spirit, for so gigantic have been the results of their fraud upon the world, they stand aghast at the probable consequences to the race should their dishonesty and disgrace be known upon the earth.

Hence, they seek in all manner known to deceivers to prevent a knowledge of the truth reaching the earth from the spiritual world, and, by a wholesale denunciation of spiritual manifestations, seek to prevent the world of mortals from ascertaining the foundation of the dogmas formerly taught as spiritual truth by them upon earth.

In this contest the spirit world of India has a deep interest, for from her came the first revelation that broke the power of the Christian hierarchy in the world of spirit as well as mortal life. It will continue until the people of earth know the truth about their gods, and whether they belong to the mystic realm of imagination or the more palpable sphere of deliberate fabrication.

The Christian world has the latter for the source of its faith, while the Oriental nations have drawn largely upon the former; but when the truth about each is seen in its true light, it will be evident why the people of India have not substituted Christian superstition for Hindoo philosophy, and why the latter is making such headway in the lands where the former has long held sway.

It may seem as if there should be some deference paid to the men who are trying to propagate the Christian ideas in India, but the ideas themselves are not essentially new or worthy of special attention by its people.

Ere I close this chapter upon the nature of the Christian deity, I ought to refer to one characteristic of those followers of him that is specially worthy of notice, although it is not specially confined to those of his faith alone, viz.: The great credulity of the masses of those countries in accepting the divinity of their man-god. Their priesthood are equally ignorant of the impossibility of their god being born out of the usual course of nature, but such is their superstitious credulity that they teach the avatarship in this particular form with an earnestness unknown in India save among the most superstitious devotees of the gods. The Christian world stakes its hopes of eternal salvation upon this priestly fabrication, and teaches it with a zeal that surpasses the comprehension of earthly wisdom.

In reality their god was born the same as other mortals, and lived and died in the same manner as all mortals would under the same circumstances; but the tales that came from the East, that were but mistaken translations of Oriental metaphor, were accepted by these ignorant people as literal truths. Hence their god has all the distinguishing traits of Sakya Muni, coupled with much of the philosophic wisdom of Egypt and Greece in the palmy days of the latter nation, so that the Christian world is but an evolution of the Oriental in its religious worship, yet not even able to comprehend the subtle thought that the East sought to embody in its mystical language. For spiritual life and spiritual thought must have their own time for a perfect evolution, and the religion of the West has never had the power to rise above the savage superstitions that clouded the Oriental thought when translated into its barbarous language.

In fact, so low were they in the scale of an intellectual spirituality that they conceived the idea from some savage or ignorant mind that the Supreme Om sent his only begotten son into the earthly life that he (the Son) might be killed, so that justice should be satisfied and their god vindicated from the charge of cruelty in the wholesale destruction of the human race.

This is the basis of the theology of the Christian world, and it is only where the wisdom of the Buddha refutes it that the Christian faith has any claim to be considered a religion of heavenly origin, yet the Buddhahood is attained but by few among that people.

Therefore, O sons of India, I come to say to you that the Christian's god is of the same nature as your own avatars, whom you have worshiped in vain for ages. They are not worthy of your adoration, nor should you seek unto them as if they held the keys of life eternal for you, or any soul. The avatars are not the embodied gods of other ages, but the more perfectly born and spiritually enlightened of your own life, and when

India ceases to expect her gods to deliver her, she will rise in the power of a new life to break the chains of every grade of oppression.

She has the gods in her own mortal children that can be the means of her deliverance, and when her children learn that the true gods of a people are from the people, they will no longer bow at the shrines of departed spirits, but lift the soul to the heights of divine contemplation, and receive the celestial light that comes to the soul at peace with itself and the Supreme.

Even the Christain world can have this light, and it is breaking through the dense clouds of ignorance and superstition that long have enveloped its people, and they are learning something of the true nature of the soul and its immortal destiny.

Despise not the light that comes to India from the Western world when it comes freed from the taint of the superstition of creedalism. It is the Buddhahood coming to them according to the Vedantic prophecies, and the West is to rejoice in its blessings as well as the hosts of India.

They know not its source, nor are they yet able to receive it in all its splendor, for their spiritual birth is not yet, although they imagine the quickening process that reaches so many is the birth unto Nirvana. In their spiritual darkness they connect it with the Buddhahood and imagine themselves enlightened, but they see not, nor can they hardly discern the voice of the spirit, so imperfect has been their spiritual evolution in the mental darkness of the past ages.

Therefore, for a while, they must remain in the mental environment in which they are being spiritually gestated, but the time of their birth will come, and then they will wonder at the mistakes they have made in their childish efforts to teach the nations of the East the nature of the spiritual life. Like children they are to be treated by the sons of Brahm, and as children outgrow the thoughts and ideas of childhood, so will the people of the West learn to regard their present crude and ignorant theories of the Divine nature, and discard them for the wisdom and benevolence which the sages of India taught the philosophers of the West centuries before the Christians' God was born, and which in reality made the better part of the Christian religion a possibility among the savage and bloody nations in which it has existed since its formulation from the systems of previous generations.

## CHAPTER IX.

### THE TRUE THEOSOPHY.

Within the memory of the past generation there has been a great evolution of spiritual thought among the Western nations which has had its influence in paving the way for the reception of a higher type of religious ideas than belonged to their ancient theology.

This epoch in their religious history began with the introduction of more liberal ideas of the nature of their Trinity, and was first formulated in the denial of the divinity of their embodied god and the substitution of him as the greatest religious teacher of his age and generation.*

This explanation of the Christian godhead was an improvement upon the extremely superstitious teachings of the ancient fathers of their faith, but it fell short of a complete analysis of the subject, for the true story of his life was not known, and the composition of the ideas upon which the mythical Savior of the Christian world was fabricated was a mystery.

The early Christian fathers or their immediate descendants were responsible for this, for in the fabrication

---

*The great spiritual wave of liberal ideas which swept over America, and culminated in the separation of the liberal from the orthodox interpreters of the scriptures, was ever a source of perplexity to the Christian sects who still clung to the barbaric theology of Calvin or Luther. A similar influx is still pushing its way Westward and sweeping away the idea of the sanctity of superstitious interpretations of any doctrine, and gradually unfolding the greater beauties of a natural evolution of all powers.—B.

of the tales regarding their deity they copied freely from the legends current in the Oriental world concerning the old gods, and save in the substitution of the mild and peaceful doctrines of Sakya Muni for the licentious intrigues of the Egyptian and Roman deities, the Christian system did not vary essentially from the religions it superseded.

But in the propagation of the beneficent ideas of Sakya Muni the Western world obtained its first intimation of the true Theosophy or wisdom of the Divine Nature. Sakya Muni had instructed his disciples that peace, not war, was the true policy to insure earthly and spiritual blessedness, and the nations of the West were so given to war that the preaching of a gospel of peace as a message from the gods was so opposed to the savage nature and moral and political measures of that people that it was long ere it was welcomed as a true system, except by the very learned or the extremely poor and ignorant, who were tired of the oppression that war engendered.

Hence, when the disciples of Sakya Muni came from the East, bearing the higher light of the spirit world, they found some opposition as well as welcome, but they had the satisfaction of seeing their ideas adopted to some extent and placed among the sacred writings of the West, although they were modified somewhat to suit the temper of the age and generation to whom they came.*

*The writings of the ancient fathers of the church abound in much that seems fanatical and absurd to us of this age, but they have had a great influence, modifying the savage disposition of the nations to whom they were given. While they reflect the thoughts of a priesthood tinged with superstition and ignorance, they probably were an improvement upon the licentious intrigues that pre-

Those writings in after ages became the basis of the Christian theosophy, which differed from the Indian in this, that it admitted of no hope of change after the physical death, whereas the ideas of Sakya held that by the attainment of Nirvana the soul would not need to ever return to the sphere of earth to have another embodiment. The Christian system changed this somewhat, to correspond with the Egyptian theory of a physical resurrection and spiritual re-embodiment, after which there would be a new heaven and a new earth, to be inhabited by those who should be found worthy to obtain entrance therein.

Sakya Muni knew well of the existence of the spiritual world, and his life work was to familiarize his disciples with the idea of a blessed life in the Nirvanian heavens after death; but the crude and ignorant West could not rise to a conception of a refined spirituality, and changed his Nirvana to a material city, built of stones and paved with gold, into which was to be admitted the favored disciples of the new faith, while the myriad hosts who had preceded them were either to remain in outer darkness or be provided for in some way unknown to the souls of earth.*

vailed in the pagan temples, and in a modified degree changed the bloody sacrifices of beasts and fowls for the more humane precepts of the schools of philosophic thought.—B.

*Here is a perfectly rational explanation of the effect of the Oriental philosophy upon the barbaric mentality of the West, and why the translation of the ideas from the Orient to the West had to have a mutilation to be received. Roman civilization was brutal and bloody in its materiality. The influx of ideas of a spiritual character was met by this material environment of the savagery of the West. It had to take a material expression—hence the Christian paradise, with its city of stone and its streets of gold, the height of barbaric conception of power and beauty.—B.

The Christian world speedily closed the doors of further information upon the subject by forbidding intercourse with the spiritual spheres as both dangerous and impossible, and sank into a night of spiritual gloom that has not yet been dispelled with all their boasted light of revelation from the source of Eternal Wisdom.

In doing this, they laid the foundations for that spiritual subservience to a priesthood that has ever striven to keep them ignorant of the truth and subordinate to the deductions of a type of mentality that knows nothing of developed spiritual powers; and that has never been able to rise above traditional interpretations of the ideas which were living truths to their original exponents.

The Western world has struggled for centuries to attain spiritual knowledge and power by ignoring the only natural method whereby such knowledge and power can be attained. Its priesthood, ignorant, and conscious of their lack of power, are cowardly opponents of the only class that has ventured to explore the forbidden realm, and who find that Christian dogma concerning it is almost totally false.

Hence, in the Christian world, spiritual science is viewed askance, and Christian ignorance is taught as divine wisdom. Many of Christian people are either superstitious devotees of an unknown God or skeptical disbelievers of the whole subject. They erect their temples and maintain a host of teachers, but the taught are left in spiritual darkness as to any proof of a spiritual life, and if they obtain it they do so by seeking light outside the channels which their religious teachers have instituted for the spiritual enlightenment of the race.

This being the situation of the Christian world, it became a necessity that there should be a revelation of a different character from the spiritual world, or the faint remnants of spirituality might be obscured in the dense darkness that envelops that people who fail to grasp the full signification of the subject. India had her spiritual evolution centuries before the Western nations knew of a spiritual idea above the plane of savages or barbarians. Her highest spiritual doctrines culminated in the ideas taught by such enlightened minds as Capilya and Sakya Muni. The spiritual life of the nation rose to the apprehension of a Divine Power that was impersonal and universal in its beneficence.

This interpretation of the Supreme was far in advance of the savage or barbarous theology of the sacrificial type, and burst upon the mortal comprehension with the vividness of a divine revelation. It was hardly worthy of this consideration, but to the minds benighted by ignorance or degraded by crime it was the signal of a new interpretation of Divinity itself.

This wisdom was called the Divine life in the Indian phraseology, or the Buddhahood. In the West, it was termed Theosophia or the wisdom of the gods. Only those anointed with it could claim spiritual illumination, and those who could attain it were to be forever exempt from the further connection with the mental atmosphere of earthly thoughts or earthly influence. To the seeker after spiritual attainments, it was represented as the goal of human effort, and to this day it is taught in more or less crude forms throughout the Christian and Heathen worlds.*

*There are scores of people to whom this spiritual enlightenment comes who never express outwardly the great changes it makes in

Where priestly dogma has not deliberately substituted for it the ceremonial form or the more vivid symbolism, it touches all minds upon the same plane of development with similiarity of thought or likeness of spiritual experience. Neither Christian nor Heathen has a monopoly of it, however, and, the wisdom of the divine order cheers all hearts to whom it comes with the blessedness of a conscious approval by the Supreme Author of all life The Christian world imagines it has a monopoly of this conscious spirituality, but its power in reality is so low and undeveloped that it may be said of it, that except among the higher castes or classes the existence of the spiritual nature is unknown. They were slow to adopt the idea of a conscious spiritual presence, and have hardly yet been able to recognize the universality of spirit, or its development among all nations upon parallel lines.*

Hence their spiritual wisdom is hardly worthy of the name Theosophia and their definitions of the Divine nature partake too much of the crudest speculation as

their mental atmosphere, but whose faces show the presence of an inner light that illuminates the pathway they tread, however rugged it may be. They are not dependent upon human definitions of its nature, nor are they disturbed by the denial of those less enlightened as to its existence. Such souls have entered the path, and will reach Nirvana ere they pass beyond the bounds of mortal life.

* The belief among Christian theologians as to the darkness of Heathen peoples has been a great stimulus to missionary effort to enlighten them, but the fact that spiritual light touches all people who have a certain degree of mental unfoldment is not generally known by them. As they had their spiritual unfoldment under the Christian definition of the term, they supposed that it was only under that system spiritual light came to earth, and so have expended much unnecessary zeal in behalf of the Heathen world.—B.

to origin or purpose in the work of cosmic creation. To them only, the Supreme Creator has made provision for the welfare of the few, while the great masses perish or are hopelessly condemned to eternal suffering. Their God has left no alternative to be considered, and the culmination of Christian theology is the deduction that the Divine wisdom utterly failed in its efforts to redeem or perfect its work in the creation of immortal beings.

This is far from the teachings of the true Theosophia (Theosophy). That declares that the Divine mind is both omnipotent and omniscient. It also affirms that its beneficence is equal to all the demands upon it for every type or form of being that exists. It says there can be no ultimate failure in the designs of planetary or any other life, and while it is not arbitrary, it affirms that all this is to be wrought by the power of the Almighty in and through the processes of spiritual law.

It penetrates the spheres of spirit, and perceives how the same essential principles prevail there as in the first sphere of evolutionary form, and declares that life being universal, progress must be eternal. It touches the secret springs of spiritual action, and traces the evolution of spirituality from its incipient stages until it ends in a perfect comprehension of the spiritual nature.

This is the declaration of Theosophy, the fruit of Indian metaphysical discovery, viz.: That all life is of God, and all life is in God (in the idiom best expressed in the tongues of the Western world), and that no life can perish without God himself be destroyed.

The theologians of the West are unable to grasp this thought in its entirety and call it Pantheism, but in their ignorance of spirituality as it is they have never fathomed in any degree the tremendous significence of their own basis of spiritual thought as personified in their Trinity. Their Holy Spirit is the nearest translation they could give to the Sanscrit Om, but with the perversity of ignorance they have placed it last in the order although it should have been first, and the controlling power of their Father, Son and Devil.

In their reversal they lost the true significance of each in the symbols from which they copied them, and have never known the meaning of the terms embodied in their barbarian theories of deity. They lost the Divine wisdom and have never regained it, for they were too proud to acknowledge their ignorance and too ignorant to seek for knowlege in the only land and nation that held the true key to the ancient symbolism Hence they adopted a spurious god, a defective creed and a ridiculous system of theology, to cope with the overwhelming power of the true Theosophy.

# CHAPTER X.

## THE SYMBOLISM OF THE ANCIENT WORSHIP.

When the missionaries of the Western nations came to India they were horrified at the respect paid to the images in the temples by which the ancient teachers sought to convey to the lower castes ideas of the principles that exist in spirit and mortal life. These images they pronounced idols worthy of destruction, for to them they conveyed a meaning entirly different from that intended by the ancient teachers. The source of life could only be symbolized by the organs of generation, which the Christian world has taught as obscene by nature, and the linga and yoni are to their minds the symbols of lust and depravity. This was not so intended by the teachers of the ancient faith, and it is curiously significant that the ball and cross with which the priests of Christian temples adorn their houses of worship are but modifications of the ancient symbolism whereby India sought to express the source of life to mortal comprehension. The Christian world put the linga and yoni at the top of their temples to this day, without knowing that in so doing they have only veiled the phallus which they denounce as tending to the deification of lust and debauchery.*

---

*This Oriental way for accounting for the Christian symbolism has been disputed by many devotees of the entire originality of Christian system. But the shrewd critics of the East have long been acquainted with the device of conveying ideas by symbols, and under any disguise they seem to see the similarity of design to

Of the other symbols that stand in the temples which represent the various gods of India, I can only say that they all exemplify the specific ideas which belong to some special system that the tolerant spirit of Hindooism has allowed to spread, or from the worship of decarnated spirits who love to be worshiped on earth by the ignorant and superstitious people there. Accordingly, they have impressed their thoughts upon the sensitive minds of the ignorant, and through the power of impression have weighed down the minds of many millions with fear and reverence of spiritual vengeance should their vengeance be neglected; but like their conterparts in the Western nations, they have no real power over those who fear them not. The goddess Doorgha or the goddess Kali* are as powerless in reality to help or harm the soul of the intelligent as the devil of the Christian world, which exists only in the imagination with which superstition has peopled the spiritual life.

The charge is boldly made, that India has lost its spiritual light through subservience to the deities whose symbols express all the phases of human passion and animality. This is only true in a limited degree, for India went down in the grade of spiritual enlightenment when she mistook the symbolism for the ideas it was intended to convey, and her degradation came when she

their own system. From the fact that Christianity is a compound of various other systems, the symbolism reflects a varied constituency and the Hindoo may not be far wrong in his deductions.—B.

*Doorgha and Kali were two ancient deified personifications of the feminine powers in nature. Their worship reflects the mental savagery that came from the primitive races of ancient India. They do not belong to the Aryan races, although tolerated by the Brahmin priesthood, along with the other gods.

forsook that high mental interpretation of the symbols for the superstitious reverence of the images as the resident forms of the spiritual power.*

Many of the Christian temples have the images of the reputed founder of their faith, and their worshipers bow in adoration before them, but they resent the imputation that they worship the image, and in reality they only use it to call more vividly to the mind the personal God which they adore; so that, if a charge of idolatry is preferred by these Western barbarians against the worship of the Oriental nations, it is of a similar character to the symbolism by which they express their divinities to the eye of the ignorant devotees.

These people of the West are grossly ignorant of the nature or use of symbols. Many of them have an hereditary opposition to their use, and suppose that they were forbidden by their God in the ancient code, which they still reverence. But they do not know that the code of laws which they ascribe to Moses was copied from the ancient laws of Zoroaster, and Menu of India, and was afterwards made the basis of the monotheistic worship of the West. Their later priesthood took these writings as a basis of doctrine, and incorporated them with the symbolism that prevailed among the Greeks, and from them compiled the code of ancient

* This superstitious regard for the emblems is not confined to Heathen peoples. In the Catholic communion, the elevation of the host, and the fancied translation of the bread and wine into the veritable body and blood of a God, is as gross a superstition as ever was held among the most idolatrous heathen nation in existence. But the Christian priesthood of that order are as literal interpreters of the dogma as the most devout Hindoo that ever bowed at the shrine of Kali or dipped himself in Ganges' sacred waters to insure eternal blessedness.—B.

and modern dogmas that is now regarded as a sacred revelation, but they have not changed the symbols in essential particulars. Even their embodied form of a God exhibits the features of Sakya Muni, and their bloody crosses reflect the savagery of their primitive worship of blood and human sacrifice.

Their saints are the lesser deities, which correspond to the spirits worshiped in India as subordinate gods; and they have divided the heavens of the West by lines that correspond with the jurisdiction of the creeds and sects, which reflect the varied thoughts of their ignorant teachers.

For these apostles of the Christian faith themselves are not aware of the true nature of spiritual powers, yet they imagine themselves competent to enlighten the world by the artificial torches which they construct out of the material given from the Oriental nations. Where they have retained their faith in the Supreme Om they have made some progress, but where they have modified or mixed it with the imagery of the symbols, they have retrograded or been seriously retarded in their development of the spiritual nature.

Yet with all their pretensions to knowledge of spiritual life from their so-called divine revelations, the existence of a spiritual life is taught by them to be incapable of proof, and their entrance upon it after death to be entirely problematical.*

*The reluctance with which the Christian church receives testimony of a character to settle the vexed question of the immortal nature of the soul is observed in its treatment of all who have become recipients of spiritual gifts. The possession of clairvoyance or the claim to the knowledge of spiritual powers is evidence

Such instructors are incapable of interpreting the symbolism of India, and their ideas relative to it are on a par with their ignorance of the symbolism of their own faith.

There is one curious result of this ignorance witnessed in the spiritual world which accounts for much that perplexes the students of spiritual phenomena in the material life. The Christian priesthood, (chiefly of the Catholic faith, as well as some Prostestant sects,) after their transition to the life of spirit cling to the errors of their earthly ideas, and strive to realize their hopes of an exclusive heaven. They find themselves unable to control any minds save those equally ignorant or of an inferior intelligence, and as they cannot control the wise in spirit life they strive to close the doors of any intelligence regarding the life of spirit from reaching the mind of mortals. By so doing, they can populate their sphere of the spirit world with a class of spirits that still regards them as oracles of wisdom, and for a season hold them in allegiance.

But their devotees soon tire of this repressive and restricted sphere of life, and, when intelligent enough to break away, soon leave them for a more intelligent and less deceptive society. For deception is the only power the priesthood of any people can exercise to retain their allegiance. The very office as exercised upon earth is an imposition upon the intelligence of man, and when the mind outgrows it, the god recedes and the priest departs.

---

enough to exclude the claimant from Christian fellowship and insure his condemnation from the authorized representatives of its creedal system.—B.

It would have left India long ago had the people risen in their intellectual power and had their spiritual gods been of a high order; but they are not, and despite the efforts of the older teachers to break the power of superstition, the despotism of the hierarchy in spirit is still felt upon earth, holding the people in mental bondage and preventing the spread of a knowledge of truth and wisdom of a higher spiritual order.

## CHAPTER XI.

### THE ERROR OF THE DOCTRINE OF REINCARNATION AS TAUGHT BY THE THEOSOPHISTS OF EARTH.

I have alluded in another place to what were the original ideas which became the basis of the present doctrine of the reincarnation of the spirit as now taught upon earth, and think it well to write further about it, as the mischief wrought by it in India has been almost beyond compute.

I have said that it only meant, in the most ancient ages, the principles by which the forming spiritual powers of earth should be perpetually reproduced in all ages, after the planet had once become able to evolve them, and I think it wise to state again in positive terms the reasons why the idea of re-embodiment of the individual in earthly relations must be beyond the province of natural law.

Notwithstanding one of the ablest writers* upon the Oriental system of Buddhism has sought to connect it with the principles of evolution, an understanding of the office of planetary life will soon expose the sophistical ideas that are inwoven with the truth, and leave the mind free to proceed upon its evolutionary pathway without the fear of having to retrace its steps to tread the earthly pilgrimage again.

The simple truth about planetary life in its first stages is, that the entity which survives death is really a product of the planetary relations of the elements

*A. P. Sinnett.

and gets its inception there. If it be forcibly detached, it can be magnetically attached to kindred spiritual entities in the form, and obtain life experience through that relation, but it has no power to go back to the primitive status or to become re-embodied at the expense of the embryotic life, and nature most emphatically refuses to permit it.

The great trouble with our modern Indian teachers is, that they fail to conceive of the eternity of matter* as well as spirit, and also fail to connect the two as correlatives in the universal cosmos. By so doing, they miss the knowledge of the inception of the spirit, and vaguely suppose it gets its original impetus from the universal impersonal spirit which seeks to express itself through matter to obtain knowledge that it could not gain elsewhere.

These metaphysical teachers of reincarnation of the individual spirit have had to meet many objections and much speculative questioning, but their chief reliance has been and still is that Karma is the cause of reincarnation, and when a good Karma is obtained they will not need to repeat the experiences of earth further.

Now it is well to go a little further into the consideration of the idea of Karma, and see if it presents any good basis for the theory of rebirth into conditions

* Perhaps it would be well to state, that the *a priori* method of reasoning common in the Oriental world is the cause of their attributing everything in nature to the direct control of a spirit. Matter in the fourth dimensional capacity has a correlative expression but not a clear definition in the language, and the confusion of thought engendered is quite noticeable when one tries to follow the ideas of the Indian philosophy in its present form. Some theosophists claim much more than they can prove at present, but the mark of the priest is on them in some form.—B.

that necessarily must be extremely likely to produce a bad Karma * If the experience of earthly life has not been able in its first influence upon the embryotic spirit to give it a good Karma, will the continuation of rebirths into the same or similar conditions be likely to improve the spirit as surely as to detach its thoughts and desires from that state as much as possible?

Now the law of spiritual unfoldment is this, that the better the conditions the wiser and purer the life, and while it may be necessary for the spiritual entity to lay its foundation in planetary life, the sooner it can escape from bad conditions there the more likely it will be to have a beautiful development. It may have to stay in the mortal environment for a season to perfect the form powers, but when that is once accomplished no necessity exists for further imprisonment upon earth, for all that earth can teach is what pertains to the physical senses rather than to the spiritual life, and to condemn a spirit to return to it after once having had its nature developed in that direction would be to degrade rather than exalt the soul, nor could anything be gained by it †

* The vagaries that follow the adoption of this idea as truth are strikingly seen in the idea that the final redemption from a bad Karma is to be obtained by a transition from earth in infancy. Of course this is only another of the fallacious ideas that error breeds when it obtains the ascendancy in the mind, for while nature enters a most marked protest against early death, Karma demands it. India has suffered terribly by the perversion of this as well as other false ideas, and infanticide has had to be suppressed by the strong hand of the civil government —B.

† Spirits of the scientific order never indorse the advisability of early death, and aver that until the embryotic spirit has obtained the necessary development of earth life, it must remain in the magnetic environment of earth. This gives it all the experience needed, and effectually disposes of the theories of a spiritual rebirth

Nature has provided the most ample means for the spiritual influx of thoughts to earth, and any spirit can avail itself of them, but to cling to the ideas of sense which pertain to earthly life is to invite the animal rather than the spiritual to obtain ascendency.

The original Karma idea was, that the soul would have to expiate in its experiences the effect of all conditions through which it would have to pass from the realm of unconscious being to the perfect development of all its powers. It was perceived by the wiser teachers of India that the spiritual influx from the lower spheres of spirit betokened a bad Karma, and that it was not possible for the spirituality of a low order to perfect itself except through a series of mental experiences or evolutions from one plane of thought to another of higher degree, and in the metaphorical expressions of the language the idea of a rebirth was used to designate this process. At first it was taught to the primitive disciples as a spiritual experience and was never understood in any other sense until a debased priesthood arose and gave the literal interpretation which has been taught in India for many generations.*

By the law of spiritual evolution, the spirit once having had its formative stages in earthly or planetary

into antenatal life. It is nature asserting her rights, which no power less than hers can deprive one of, but she can do it without disturbing the general equilibrium of either world.—B.

* The hand of the priest is ever potent to *improve* the teachings of the philosopher. Here a perfectly natural process of soul unfoldment upon a spiritual plane is perverted and dragged into the mire of sensual life to sustain the prerogatives of a priesthood. It is a wonder that the crafty swindlers did not offer a free passage into Brahm by the payment of a fee, but that was reserved to the priesthood of the Christian world.—B.

life has no more necessity for returning to that condition than the developed bird has to reenter the shell of the embryotic period, for the earth experiences at best are but formative, and, as far as being of any great value except in the necessities of the embryotic stages of life, may be said to be detrimental rather than to be desired.

Planets are a necessity in the supreme economy to organize the elements into conscious entities known as spirits, but beyond that function they have no essential purpose of a spiritual character. They have ever been the nurseries of the embryotic forms of spirits, and fill a great office in this respect, but they are far from being a necessary factor in the higher gradations of spiritual power; and when it has been necessary to raise the grade of the spiritual environment of their peoples, it has had to be done by influx that excites the hopes of the soul to escape from the trammels of form life, rather than by teaching that a necessity exists to return and repeatedly pass through its experiences.

There is an influx of thought upon this subject pouring in upon the planet earth to-day, that has its origin in the mental bias of Hindoo thought of the present age, and that bodes much trouble if it be not checked. India has steadily sunk in the grade of her spiritual powers because of it, for in place of the pure doctrines of the ancient Vedantic system the priestly perversion is taking its place as the original ideality. In Europe and America, the teachers of the wisdom divine are confounding the moral sentiments that are the basis of spiritual unfoldment with the superstitions engendered by the priesthood, and ere the people of those countries are aware they will be invaded by the hosts of the lower Asian heavens, who still are seeking re-embodiment, and a carnival of licentiousness may be inaugurated that will sink those countries as low in the scale as India has ever been.

For the spiritual thought of a people is the standard of its grade in knowledge, and to a soul imbued with the idea of reincarnation to escape the consequences of a bad Karma all avenues are legitimate, and a parentage of adultery is as welcome as the doorway of wedlock.*

It is for this reason I would send the warning note to the world of the West, that while they admit the ideas of India as far as they open the gates of knowledge of the spiritual world, to discriminate between the pure doctrines of the Vedas and the fanciful theories of the ignorant and crafty pretenders who close the doors in all lands to the influx of intelligent spiritual ideas.

The Western world has had a deluge of Oriental creedalism to counterbalance its own crude conceptions of the Divine nature, but neither formula has proven sufficient to protect its believers from flagrant imposition in the name of their gods. The Oriental influx is seized upon by the souls in darkness or despair, and labeled by various names as well as taught by numerous schools, each of whom only appreciates a portion of the truth.

Some of them deny the individual existence of any

*The Theosophical schools with their secret initiation ceremonies and mysterious mutterings of Karmic wrath may not be aware that the Western nations have a spiritual guardianship that sees through their flimsy pretexts; but a power exists that can tell all the secrets which they so carefully veil, and which they hesitate not to villify if it suits their purposes. To flood the West with the reincarnation theories is to invite an irruption of the vilest grades in spirit life, and no wonder that the higher spheres of spirit are averse to it.—B.

thing but the impersonal Supreme, and imagine they will be absorbed in the Divine ocean of spirit upon their transition to the world of soul life, losing consciousness and individuality. Others are sure that the spiritual world can have no direct influx into the sphere of conscious life upon earth, and teach that such an idea is delusion or dangerous. Others, again, are so anxious to become united to the godhead that they forget the great law of spiritual unfoldment, and seek to hurry matters, generally ending in disappointment, or shame and disgrace.

Fanaticism is slowly rearing its hideous face in the spiritual movement, and the most absurd dogmas regarding the power of the spirit to control the material forces are freely advocated, not because the disciples are not honest, but because they know not the nature of the laws governing either. The most irrational ideas of the control of spiritual powers by the will of ignorant embodied souls are advanced, and the experiments made by the most intelligent minds in spirit to demonstrate principles are supposed to be in the regular order of evidence to support the theories of extravagant visionaries.

Perhaps no more difficult lesson has ever been learned upon earth, than the hopelessness of its ignorance of what really pertains to its spiritual nature and the true position it holds in the universal life.*

* The amount of intelligent ignorance current upon earth is one of the problems that eternity alone can solve. There are societies and systems innumerable for the study of the occult forces, but hardly any two of them can agree touching the nature of the spirit or the true methods of its enfoldment. Even the wisest minds fail here to discriminate between the natural laws and the artificial theories that pertain to it.—B.

It would, indeed, be a sorrowful fate for humanity if it was bound by the decrees of the spiritual magnates of earth. It would have a hopeless destiny were it compelled to follow the pathway that Hindoo or Christian theology had marked out for it in the Divine economy. But fortunately it is not bound to obey either any further than they follow the natural law of spiritual evolution.

That law does not call for the return to the environment of earth after its escape from the atmosphere of earthly thoughts, nor does it ever need to express itself again in the realm of earthly embodiment. Its pathway to Nirvana is away from earth, and happy the soul who is freed from the idea of ever having to tread the path through mortal life again.*

Gautama taught truly in this, and could India emancipate herself from the tyranny of the idea of reincarnation, she would rise in the scale of spiritual enlightenment far higher than she rose in the age of the Vedas or when Capilya or Gautama led her hosts toward the heavenly paradise. She must do this or she must remain the prey to vile superstitions, and her moral nature be degraded by the mental influx of myriad hosts who strive in vain to realize the truth of the dogma.

The Western nations have been the prey of a senseless belief in a return to the physical body, but not

*Compare the moral power of this thought with the idea that life is a ceaseless round of incarnations upon the various planets, and weigh well the difference. One exalts the spiritual consciousness to the highest heavens, while the other condemns the victim to perpetual despair. For the thought of return in spirit cannot be forgotten, and it is only when the soul experiences the emancipation from it that it can soar onward into the realms of Nirvana.—B.

through the process taught so many years in India, and although the numerous hosts of her ignorant children hover over the earth awaiting the resurrection morn, yet they can do but little harm compared with the souls whose thought is felt upon the earth as they strive to impress the mortals there to furnish avenues for the spirit to enter earth again to expiate a bad Karma. The societies forming in the West for the study of Hindoo thought should be aware that the projection of thought upon earth by a concentrated effort of the will must have its effect there, and if that thought be upon a plane of error, it may be long ere its effect will be removed. Therefore I speak thus positively about the subject of the reincarnation of the spirit.

A Hindoo of the ages so long ago that my name is forgotten; but one who has been worshiped as an incarnation of Brahm, I claim the right to speak to India and to the world, warning them not to trust in the wisdom of man, whose interpretation of the laws of spirit must be vain, until he has arrived to that degree of knowledge whereby he knows the nature and office of spirit and form in the spheres of universal being.

# CHAPTER XII.

## THE ORIGIN OF THE SPIRITUAL ENTITY.

The world of mortal life has ever been the subject of speculative inquiry by the thinkers of all ages, and from the earliest periods of conscious mentality the origin of the spirit has occupied the attention of the most learned in earthly knowledge.

India was the first nation to develop a school of metaphysical study, and she was the most profound student of the varied powers that enter into the structure of sentient life She saw that life belonged to a regular order of physical relations, and she also saw that connected with it was a realm of life beyond the physical which had much to do with determining the status of thought prevalent in that relation, and upon that premise she built her great doctrine of the immortal nature of the spirit.

Clustered around this central point of fact has been gathered the web and woof of fictitious drapery that conceals the truth from the beholder and presents a spectacle of illusive theories which have been accepted by the students of the modern age as the genuine Indian philosophy According to this latter school of pundits, the ancient sages formulated a system whereby the worlds, visible and invisible, could ever act and react upon each other with definite and tangible effects, that were subject to human comprehension and subordinate to human manipulation. Briefly stated this system is, that all individual souls owe their origin to the differentiation of One Supreme Soul who presides over and permeates the universe. All these subordinate parts of the Supreme Spirit are themselves but as individual drops in the great Ocean of Spirit from which they came, and to which they return in the cyclic periods of eternity, losing and regaining consciousness as they pass through the conditions of planetary unfoldment, but liable to extinction in the universal abysm of absorption by the Supreme if the life stages fail to produce a perfect Karma.*

Under this system, the spiritual entity only enters planetary life to acquire experience, and passes from one planet to another in the grand cyclic waves of life energy, as it flows from one planetary system to another. By this theory, the spirit entity has its organic functional powers previous to its entrance upon planetary life, and in that stage is termed an elemental.

Now, if this idea of the spiritual nature or origin of the individual is true, it places the office of planetary existence, as a nursery of conscious intelligence, entirely out of the question, and calls for more light than the teachers of the doctrine have yet thrown upon it; for the birth and development of intelligent mentality follows after the gestation and birth of the form, and as the intelligent spirit becomes the fruitage of developed planetary conditions, one naturally considers

---

* The reader of occult literature is often puzzled to see how the differentiation of the spirit is accounted for upon the theory of a segregation of the Infinite spirit. The evolutionary theory, upon the other hand, gives a rational hypothesis of the organization of non-conscious forces into sentient relations through planetary formulation. Probably the true nature of the Supreme mentality of the Infinite has not been accurately defined by even the wisest metaphysicians in either realm yet.—B.

whether it is not contemporary with, or an evolution of, planetary life itself.

If it be so, then there is another reason than the Oriental theory for planetary existence, for without planets the great universal ocean of spirit cannot be expressed in individual form or concentrated in personal reflection of the primate principles of spirit. To do this, there has to be the segregation of the individual drops; but if the elemental theory is correct, the individual soul needs no planetary existence to express itself, and would have little to gain by it.

But Nature, that never labors in vain, does not uphold the elemental theory in her processes of planetary life. In her alembic she distills the essences of the elements, and draws forth new combinations in every age and stage of planetary being. She wastes nothing, and if the evolutions of life and form are more imperfect in certain stages of the planet than in others, she does not cruelly annihilate the crude and undeveloped, but provides better conditions, and from the same elementary principles produces better forms and higher grades of life, until, from age to age, the life forces stored in the planet have crowned her efforts with godlike creations upon the plane of mortal existence, meanwhile withdrawing the crude forms as the more perfect absorb the energy that formerly was utilized by the primitive life entities.

For there is a strict relation between the internal forces that compose the spiritual basis of life upon the planet, and the form through which the life is expressed. The spirit of a snake or a higher reptile cannot rise much higher in the form of the snake than the conditions in which it had its primitive evolution. The other orders of animal life follow this same law, and the human race has no exemption, for its spiritual ideals are high or low according to its grade of development in the corresponding conditions of the planet at the time its ancestral types were perfected.*

Man alone has the world of planetary life to subdue to his will, but even he finds that his evolution follows along the same pathway that the other kingdoms of the planet have to pursue, viz.: The steps of a series of unfolding powers that culminate in the evolution of an intellectual spiritual being. The reptilian orders do not rise to this grade in planetary conditions, nor do the lower mammalian, but the higher orders reflect modified intellectual powers, while all must possess more or less the traits of individuality in whatever phase of planetary unfoldment they pass into the realm of spirit.

This is the reason why the Hindoo of the past ages declared life of the animal world to be sacred, and is also the source of the idea of repeated incarnations to raise the spirit to the grade of the godlike qualities of perfected mentality.

For the sages of India saw that in spirit the forms of the decarnated life of the planet all bore the impress of the more or less perfected powers of the developing life

---

* This may be denied by the advocates of spiritualization through religious influx, and many systems of faith have been based upon the possibility of effecting the civilization of the savage tribes by changing their religious ideas. While there undoubtedly is a corresponding influx from the world of spirit which aids the missionary in his labors, there is little question that the elimination of the savage or barbarous traits is a work of progressive evolution, requiring generations of culture to make any permanent impression.—B.

upon the planet, and as there was the natural magnetic interchange of mentality between the corresponding spheres in spirit and mortal life, it became easy to teach the idea of association in the spheres, and also its perversion to the theories of transmigration and reincarnation by the speculative philosophers and priesthood, that seized upon the ideas as a leverage to control the multitude through fear of the spiritual consequences if they were not duly reverenced.*

If the ideas that have been taught so many centuries in India as to the nature of the soul and the origin of life are deflections from the great parent idea, what has the world of the intellectually developed spiritual intelligence to offer to the world of mortal consciousness upon the subject?

Briefly this: The origin of conscious spirit in form begins in the planetary stages of form development. The elements there come into the correlative conditions, whereby the resultant combinations upon certain planes act in conscious relations. Those planetary conditions are as essential to this result of the interaction of the elements in form, as the lower grades of form result from the lower rates of the elements in crystallization of the rocks or cell life organisms. The spiritual entity forms from the elements seeking a higher equilibrium than the crystalline and lower organic forms; and through the steady increase of the combinatory powers of the same elements that make a planet, they make a

*The regard for animal life that even to this day has such a hold in India is but another form of the superstitous deflections from the primitive faith which causes a devout Catholic Christian to worship a relic of a saint, or regard a piece of wood as a sacred object. It is doubtful, however, if the superstition of the Hindoo is not at least as sacred as the mummery of his Christian critic.—B.

planetary form that contains within itself the pulsating forces that are able through form to express the intelligent relations which belong to the sphere of the invisible state, yet are not primarily individualized there.*

Thus through the planet, as a great reservoir battery of forces, the spiritual entity gets its inceptive life expression, and, laying its foundation in form, goes forward ever after, holding the forces in form that previously were acting mechanically or subordinate to the great universal realm of unconscious material, and without other control than general principles.†

The reader can see how easily the primitive idea of evolution of spirit individuality from the universal realm of spirit was modified to seem to give color to the present system of Buddhistic and Brahmanistic theories of the origin of the soul. It was as easy for the unscrupulous priestly orders of India to formulate their creeds and philosophies upon this basis, as it was for the Christian world to crystallize the ignorant

*This statement as to the origin of the spirit entity is clear and explicit enough to satisfy any one as to what is meant. If the supreme mind is impersonal the subordinate ones are not, and their organization from the elements through planets seems to account for the existence of the latter. It puts an effectual damper upon the theory of pre-existent consciousness in form, and agrees quite well with natural law as expressed in planetary life.—B.

†The necessity of planetary conditions for the evolution of spirit entities may be seen in the regular law of planetary unfoldment. Even the first evolution of form from the elements, as seen in the crystal, bears witness to the basic principles of all entities, for the most minute form of crystallization only becomes capable of form by the principles of atomic balance, whereby primordial substance changes from force relations to form manifestations. When the balance is high enough we have the life cell in organic forms, and by a still higher balance we have the spirit entity, which reflects

speculations of an ignorant age and give them to the world as revealed truth from the godhead. It became equally easy to build a series of religious sects upon different interpretations of the ideas in subsequent ages, until the monstrous tissue of fact and fable known as Hindooism, with its multifarious gods and shrines, took the place of the pure and primitive ideas taught by the great teachers of India in the days when the Vedas were given, and which even yet reflect much of its ancient glory.*

For India really obtained a knowledge of the essential principles that pertain to all departments of planetary life. She could not express them in the literal delineation of the Western nations, but she saw into the generic principles of form and spirit, and left a record of many truths that can only be rediscovered in the experiences of this age. She knew both Om and Brahm, and the relations that each held in universal

the different gradations of the same powers that pertain to planetary form in its first stages of unfoldment. This spirit entity belongs to the planet as much as a natural child belongs to the forms from which it received its incipient evolution, and as a spirit it must perfect its form powers in planetary conditions or not have a perfect development. This is why so many feeble spirits have to be earthbound until they outgrow the weaknesses of earth life, or, in other words, obtain a well balanced form to express power.—B.

*Mr. A. P. Sinnett, in his masterly treatise on Esoteric Buddhism, reflects the power of the combination of craft and truth which the priestly class of India are teaching as the doctrines of Gautama. While the book probably is the most elaborate and reliable on the subject given from the earthly transmission of the ancient doctrines, it bears the marks of the priesthood, and its concealed dogmas and hints stamp it as defective in this particular at least. This age has no further use for priests or their interpretations of the original doctrines.—B.

life. She touched the shores of immortal existence, and brought back to earth the essential ideas that ultimately make that sphere of being a realm of undying felicity. She lighted the torches of Grecian and Egyptian science, which raised the savages of the West to the sphere of an intellectual development in the realm of material forces unsurpassed in the history of the planet. She is the mother of the idea of the divine in the human, and to her the nations of earth will yet accord the praise or recognition of being the first to formulate a system of spiritual gradation that has never been surpassed, as well as to touch upon the lines of thought that bind planet to planet and system to system in the Universal Cosmos, and she was the first to give to earth the intelligible reasons for the existence of worlds in the economy of Creative purposes.*

Grand as has been her past, it equals not her future; for when a nation arises once to the heights of intellectual spirituality it can never fall so low as to entirely lose its position in the world of spiritual thought. Her seed, so abundantly cast upon the waters of earth, is

*Those who have studied the metaphorical statements of Indian cosmology have been struck with the remarkable coincidences of the ideas veiled in that manner with the discoveries of modern science. When they speak of the golden womb from which the Sun god issued, it is only a poetical method of teaching the great principle of planetary gestation in the solar stage of planetary formation. Veiled in the darkness of creative powers, the great planets of the siderial system literally had a golden womb in which they came into cosmic existence, and the masterly intellects of ancient India pierced the veil that shrouds creative mysteries and gave them to the world in metaphor. See "Siderial Evolution," opposite page 1.—B.

returning to her, and her life again shall arise from the dust of the past, and she shall resume her position as the mistress of all science in all the departments of being.

# CHAPTER XIII.

## THE FRATERNIZATION OF THE ORIENTAL AND OCCIDENTAL NATIONS.

The influx of Oriental philosophy into the mental environment of the Western nations has ever been fraught with considerable effect upon the mental equilibrium of all to whom it has come as a distinct power.

From the time when Pythagoras sought the shrines of India to learn of the science of the soul, until the scholars and sages of the present generation that are following in his footsteps, India has ever held the key of all thought in her grasp, and if reluctant to open the treasuries of her storehouse, nevertheless has had the treasures within her possession, although despised and condemned by her ignorant despoilers.

England might send her fleets and armies to subdue and plunder a peaceful people, but England could never wrest from the sacred caste of India the greatest of its possessions, viz., the accumulated treasures of the world's intellectual achievements of prehistoric ages. It was only when India chose to bestow these priceless gifts that the world of modern civilization ever dreamed of their existence, and India never gave them up until the world of spirit had opened the gates of eternal life to the vision of the people of the Western world.

There was a good reason for this, for the people of the West were unfit to handle these treasures, nor are they yet sufficiently spiritualized to receive them but in a modified degree.

India as a nation founded her mental concepts of all life upon the demonstrated powers of the spirit in each world of its expression, and she was not one iota behind the mental development attained by any nation that ever lived upon the planet. She sought the fountain of spiritual knowledge, and, as far as obtaining that knowledge was possible in her then state of mental evolution, she went far above the schools of modern civilization, for she did not disassociate the powers of nature as expressed in the visible world from the forces of that same nature after their transition to the life eternal. She dwelt in harmony with the gods of the worlds, and the gods bestowed upon her the wisdom that gods only can bestow, and for lack of which the people of the West are groping in darkness at the shrines of priestly fabrication, and from which they can never emerge until, like the sages of India, they welcome the light which radiates from the spheres of spirit.

Her great minds may aver that the cause of planetary life is unknown and unknowable, but India knows the nature of the world builders as she knows the source from which the Ganges flows. To her mind Brahm is not beyond the power of analysis, neither is Om powerless to make his presence felt to mortals

But Indian philosophy as it comes to the West should come in its pristine purity, shorn of the fictitious drapery which long ages have enabled the symbolic expression to conceal the truth from the open vision. There is no need of secret societies for the spread of the great ideas which since the age of the Vedas have made India a distinct reservoir of spiritual wisdom. Those ideas are indeed the wisdom of the gods, but they need no priestly ministrants in this age of the world.*

They come from the world of spirit as freely now as they ever came to the great teacher in the palmy days of Sakya Muni or when the Vedas themselves were given by the wise instructors who spoke the words of Brahm. While the pundits of the modern age, both in India and in the Western world, are striving to revive the higher truths of spirit, they should not forget that with the mortals of earth the spirit hosts who linger there, earth bound by ignorance, are to rise equally in spirit by the sublime doctrines which emancipate all souls from the dominion of Agni.†

It is thus that India can be instrumental in teaching the nations as to the truth of a spiritual life that knows no limitations of beneficence and no bounds to its advancement. It is thus she is to be the connecting link between the civilization of the remote past and the

*The absurd claims of some of the theosophical schools of America to the possession of secret knowledge that cannot be communicated to the world is pointedly rebuked by this statement. To suppose that the spiritual nature of man could be subjected to the domination of a close corporation of religious teachers in this age, is to rank the intelligence of the believers with the credulity that has made heathen and Christian nations the victims of an unscrupulous priesthood. No wonder a most vigorous protest from the other world is sent to this against the subjugation of the mentality of the West to any such farcical claims to the possession of Divine knowledge or spiritual powers as held by the initiates of the Oriental dogmas. Spiritual powers and all their accompaniments seem to be more widespread than the close communion disciples of the Blavatsky school are willing to allow, and some of them do not hesitate to indulge in wholesale falsehood as a part of their system when others obtain all the secrets free of charge.—B.

†The Hindoo god of fire or the lower spheres.—B.

dawning age of a spiritual evolution that will carry the inhabitants of earth far above the plane of selfish concern for the future, and free them forever from the domination of mental as well as spiritual tyranny.

For the people of earth are bound in slavish chains of fear when they regard the world of soul life as a dark and doleful realm for any soul that ever crosses its borders. It is only dark to the undeveloped and unformed soul who, misinformed by its trusted instructors, comes to its presence unripe, and who is held in that condition until the embryotic spiritual nature can spring forth in a new birth that carries it far above the plane of earth and its surroundings.

That birth in spirit might as well be passed upon earth as to wait until the soul has left the sphere of mortal life. It must be had in one state or the other ere the intellectual powers of the soul can have their full development. When it is once effected, the soul no longer feels the influx of spirit only, but it can see the kingdom of the gods and becomes as one of them, knowing good and evil and their exact relations to each other.

The Western world has embodied this thought in its religious systems, but, like the systems of India, the thought will not follow the channel of expression merely because the individual happens to seek it there. It belongs to the universal realm of life, and every soul that exists tends toward it, and will ultimately attain it even if it misses at first the path that the great teachers marked out as leading to it. The soul must often make its own pathway, and when it does this, it is not far from the borders that lie between the mortal and the immortal life. It is a child of Brahm, and Brahm is never beyond the reach of its voice when it obeys the word of Brahm as voiced in its own consciousness.

I have spoken severely of the egotism that belongs to the different advocates of the various religious systems of earth, and I have done so because as long as that exists there is an impassible barrier between the fraternization of the different races. When nations or classes forget their original status in the world, and cultivate pride of birth, or exclusive relations toward the rest of mankind, they arouse the worst elements in themselves or others that can be excited toward producing disastrous results in the department of their spiritual welfare. In place of attracting to themselves the finer qualities of spiritual regard in all who feel their influence, they excite a chilling antagonism that freezes the life blood of the spirit, and effectually bars out all desire for aid or intercourse.

When a religious system is adopted by a sect or individual, based upon this theory, the rest of the world becomes indifferent to its existence, and naturally contemptuous of its believers. It is valueless for the mind and dies a deserved death, for it only generates hatred as long as it serves to excite any interest in others. Many of the old religions of earth perished because of this, and most of them that are left would do well to heed the lessons of the past if they would survive the righteous judgment that befalls all the systems of earth. Those only live long that fill a human necessity, and when the need is outgrown, the system naturally fades out from human consideration.

The nations of the West are imbued with the idea that Christianity is the only true system that ever existed upon earth; the followers of Mohammed are sure that none but believers in the great prophet can ever cross the bridge which leads to paradise; the disciples of Confucius are certain of a blessed reception awaiting the inhabitants of the flowery kingdom; but the sages of India know that the children of Brahm in all nations will receive the reward of faithful devotion to their highest knowledge when they pass to the life eternal, whether they bow the knee to Jesus, Allah, Joss or Brahm while in the earthly realm of being.

It is to bring about a realization of this great truth, discovered so many centuries ago, that the present world wide spiritual movement is instituted. Many concerned in it imagine they have a better right to interpret it than others who, feeling its power, are moved to voice the sentiments underlying it, but the truth is, that to no sect or nation is the work confined.

The Christian nations are being spiritualized by its power as never known before, although their priesthoods oppose its methods if outside the channels they have constructed for it to flow in The fierce son of the desert, who swears by Allah, is moved upon to be less cruel, and to consider if, after all, the rest of the world are not children of Allah, even if they know not of Mohammed as his prophet. The inhabitant of the celestial kingdom has never lost his reverence for the doctrines of the great teacher, and is more easily taught the great lesson of the universal fraternity of all races; while the pundit of India looks on in silence, wondering if the Vedantic prophecies are to be fulfilled in his day, and the nations of the earth are to become subservient to Brahm through spiritual light and knowledge.

Thus the work of illuminating the earth is going forward, and the light which once shone so brilliantly on the plains of India is again sending its beams to the utmost borders of the earth. It lights and warms the frigid creeds of barbaric Christian Europe, and fairly blazes and burns on the shores of distant America. It finds a ready welcome there, for it fills the souls of that mighty people with the knowledge of spiritual life which the barren creeds of Europe never knew or realized. It radiates the brilliancy of an intellectual enlightenment of spirit that rivals the age of Gautama, and gives to the West the dawn of the Buddhahood which never before was known to shine beyond the shores of India.

Great as has been the glory of Indian mentality, greater shall be the intellectual power of the West, for to her has come the light of the world which lighteth every man that comes into it. Grand as have been the achievements of America in the field of civil and religious emancipation. they shall be surpassed in the greater conquest of the animal by the spiritual, and the evolution of a mentality that exceeds any attainment ever made by the Oriental world.

For the Western world is the home of the spiritual philosophy, new born and newly christened, in this age of the planet. It is the planetary center where all the nations fraternize, and where, casting aside the narrow creeds and dogmas of the old world, the people rise to some comprehension of the life in spirit, where all the nations of the earth meet in peace and harmony. It is the only nation that reflects the true principles that govern the life eternal, and India, with her numerous races, when freed from the domination of foreign rulers, will find the great nation of the West her chosen ally and friend. Each represents the highest culmination of earthly attainment, and both are to stand before the world the great republics of the two hemispheres. Each had its discipline under England's power, but as America threw off the yoke when the time of her birth as a republic had come, so India in time will emerge from the thralldom of a foreign power, to become the model republic of the Oriental world.

She is not dead, nor is she to sleep in forgetfulness of her birthright forever. She is the oldest of all nations that have held their autonomy, and she belongs to the great fraternity of man in spirit, for she was the first to teach the race the principles of spiritual fraternization.

America is her child in spirit, and America will be the only child she will ever recognize as having the title to an immortal nationality. To her come the greatest of her spiritual teachers, and while the lesser lights of India emit their feeble rays upon the mortal plane, the greater souls who once taught the truth in its purity are able to speak directly, and correct the errors with which human ignorance or craft has obscured the doctrines.

The children of the West and the offspring of the East are alike precious to the souls of the great masters of India, and because of the estimation in which both are held, do the sages of former ages send their thoughts back again, to tell the people of all nations that India greets all souls as Om cares for all worlds, and that no soul can ever perish who comes into being in Brahm's world or in Om's universe.

# SKETCH OF THE LIFE OF BRAHMA

In the ancient traditions of India, we are frequently met with allusions to a certain teacher to whom was applied the term of the great Brahma. This appellation has often caused much speculation as to who was meant, for its connection with the Hindoo deity, who represents creative power, caused many to infer that the great Brahma could only mean the creator of the worlds, or the ruler of the universe.

But a better acquaintance with the metaphorical language of that country reveals the fact, that in the most ancient traditions any great character who strikingly manifested the traits of a spiritual unfoldment was termed a son of Brahm, and that there are several upon whom the application of the term Brahma was bestowed.

The Vedas are said to have issued from the four mouths of Brahma, which is a symbolical method of designating four different authors of the sacred books. Thus the mythology of ancient India grew apace, from the various traditions of the schools of philosophy and religion that clustered around the numerous incarnations of Brahm, to whom the term Brahma was indiscriminately applied, and Brahminism naturally embodied most of the ideas in modified form in its religious system.

The teacher to whom India was most indebted for her spiritual enlightenment, probably soon after the invasion of the Aryan race, is better known as the great

Brahma, from the impress he made upon the nation through his probable compilation of the Vedas. His true history is lost or obscured by traditions, but fragments of his doctrines are still preserved in some of the most striking ideas of the Vedantic philosophy.

This teacher evidently was cosmopolitan in his treatment of the different races in India, and the fine quotation that the Supreme Brahm is said to have uttered, which is often given as the highest expression of Deific benevolence, belongs to him, viz.: "Those who serve other gods in sincerity, worship me."

That unique work, *Oahspe*, has quite a full account of this teacher, and although much of it is symbolical in idea rather than literal in interpretation, it probably gives quite as good an idea of the life work of this teacher as any tradition extant. With his wife, he is represented as living a life of self-denial and hardship, that he might instruct the people in the ancient Zarathustrian faith, of belief in and obedience to Ormazd as the only true god worthy of worship.

This teacher belonged to the Semitic race, and was of obscure origin, and his true name seems to have been lost in the lapse of ages, or rather obscured by the title that overshadowed his personal characteristics.

In treating of ancient Hindoo historic characters, especially of the religious order, one has to be extremely careful in his estimates of the probable and fanciful, for the people of India have cultivated the imaginative faculties so excessively, that truth and fiction are blended so perfectly as to seem inseparable. In doing this, they seem unconsciously to have no power of discrimination between the false and the real, and live in a mental glamour that is unknown in European consciousness. Hence, they have the reputation of being incorrigable liars, when in reality they are unable to discern between what they mentally perceive as truth and what externally exists as reality.

The great teachers of India all strove to correct this defect, and especially did the teacher called the great Brahma endeavor to impress upon the people the real relations that exist in the spheres of conscious life and all their consequences to the spiritual nature. European scholarship is bringing to light the treasures of Asiatic literature, and the proper translation of the ideas embodied in it will do much toward qualifying the claims of the Western nations to the possession of exclusive religious revelation from the spiritual world. The great Brahma left in the Vedas about as distinct a record of the primitive religious ideality of India as now exists, and it is fully as worthy of confidence as the revelations upon which the Christian world basis its creedal systems. There is in the Upanishads and other ancient writings the impress of as distinct a system of Monotheistic worship, as well as a comprehensive description of the attributes of the Supreme Deity, as can be found in any sacred writing in the world.

Those who think that India has not anything of value to give to the world in this age should read Max Muller and Edwin Arnold carefully, and compare the ideality embodied in some of the sacred writings that belong to India with the system of thought that pertains to the Christian world. From the frequent allusions to the Devas and their influence upon the world of mortals, and the system of grading the gods and spirits into guardians and protectors of earth, we can see how the ancient Hindoo faith antedates Christian mythology, and corresponds in all essential points to the highest concepts of modern ideality in its definitions of the spiritual life.

That the great Brahma must have been familiar with spiritual knowledge of a high order, is evident from the spirit of the Vedantic writings, which embody the purest philosophy of the ancient world. It is not strange that the Brahmin priesthood sought to preserve a monopoly of the ideas embodied in the Vedas, and forbade the transmission of them except by oral recitation from century-to-century, although it is not improbable that ere the rise of this priesthood they might have been preserved in writing

In dealing with the perverted ideas of modern Brahminism, one has to be continually upon guard against the misconstruction of the ancient ideality, for the subtle distinction that prevails in the Hindoo mind of this age is hardly perceptible in the mentality that belongs to the early teachers who never stooped to deception or tolerated the spirit of craft. The great teachers of ancient India were famous for their simplicity of doctrines, and never can be accused of willfully mystifying the truths they sought to bestow upon their followers.

That the true history of the great Brahma must have been purposely obscured by the craft of the priesthood of subsequent ages is almost unquestionable, although in so doing the priesthood could the better conceal their deviation from the pure philosophy which he taught, and by which India rose to some realization of the sublime heights of spirituality that belonged to the system of Zarathustra.

The Vedantic prophecies, read in the light of spiritual revelations in this age, show conclusively that modern scholarship is at fault rather than Indian philosophy, and that the spiritual ideas embodied in it have a substantial foundation. They also show that the great teachers of India have always been true to their knowledge of spirituality, nor did they ever sink in the scale of inability to learn the greater truths of the life immortal and its connection with the consciousness of earth.

While many of our European and American thinkers have been active in propagating ignorance of a spiritual world as an antidote to the perverted spiritual comprehension prevalent in Christian countries, the sages of India have never been swerved from their allegiance to the transmitted faith of the Vedas, and confidence in the immortality of the spirit is still a cardinal principle of Brahminism.

It is hardly questionable if this idea is not the strongest motive power of the present age, and if it will not be the point of contact where the thought of the liberal and spiritual mind of the West will reach the religious elements of India and quicken them into a new life. Certain it is that anything less than this will not be received in India by the disciples of the great Brahma, and if this fails the Brahmin caste will ultimately be superseded by some more liberal exponents of the ideas that once made India the teacher of spiritual ideality among the nations of the earth.

## THE COMING OF BRAHMA.

Where Jumna greets the Ganges' flood,
  The ancient sage of India came,
And altars stained with human blood,
  Forever vanished through his name.

When Brahma comes, the Vedas say,
  The race of man shall have new birth;
The gloom of night be changed to day,
  The gods be seen upon the earth.

O, Sons of Light, that hour draws nigh!
  The radiant gleams of Heavenly truth
Are shining from the world on high,
  As in the hour of Brahma's youth.

Through North and South, in East or West,
  The light of Spirit fills the Earth;
No more in symbols now expressed,
  Thus Brahma has his second birth.

The Buddha shines with star-like grace,
  "It lights the hosts of Brahma's heaven,"
But Brahma lights the earthly race
  With power of mind to mortals given.

O, Sons of Brahm, this world is ours!
  No longer seek the gods of yore;
Within the soul are all the powers
  That rule the worlds forevermore.

CPSIA information can be obtained
at www.ICGtesting.com
Printed in the USA
BVHW041359050619
550259BV00006B/131/P